HOW TO WRITE
YOUR
BOOK
WITHOUT
THE FUSS

LUCY McCARRAHER AND **JOE GREGORY**

RƎTHINK PRESS

First published in Great Britain 2015
by Rethink Press (www.rethinkpress.com)

PRAISE

"Lucy and Joe have nailed it. Their enormous combined experience in every aspect of writing and publishing books shines through on every page of this very smart and very practical book."

Andrew Griffiths, international best-selling business author and International Director of Publishing for Key Person of Influence

"Getting your book published is the best way I know to get your message out to the world in a big way. If you want to make the writing process more enjoyable, get clarity on your unique message and achieve transformational results, then this book is a great place to start."

Jamie Smart, Author of #1 bestsellers *Clarity: Clear Mind, Better Performance, Bigger Results* and *The Little Book of Clarity*

"As a soon-to-be author you have a massive task ahead of you: writing your book. Lucy and Joe's book helps you to cut down on the time it takes to turn your brilliant idea into a published book you can proudly hold in your hands. They consider everything you need to think about and a lot more. If you're considering becoming an author, you need this book! I spent a lot of time researching how to get published and then discovered Lucy and Joe at Rethink Press. I was impressed by their knowledge of the publishing industry and their flexible approach to publishing, so worked with them to publish my book, *Marketing to Win*. I've recommended them to every budding author ever since!"

Jacqueline Biggs, author of *Marketing to Win* and co-founder of Brand-camp.com

"The best how-to books always inspire action rather than sit on the shelf. This manual is an indispensable guide through the thousands of decisions that go into writing and publishing your own work. The authors' advice took our book, *Insider Secrets of Public Speaking,* from a good idea to a finished article we are really proud of – and now this advice is available to everyone. It deserves to become a standard reference and makes writing a self-help book much more accessible to a wider audience."

Nadine Dereza and Ian Hawkins, Presenters and co-authors,
Insider Secrets of Public Speaking

"If you're going to write a book to position yourself as the expert in your niche, it makes sense to go to the experts in book writing and publishing to help you get the job done right. Lucy and Joe at Rethink took the first draft of my book, *Process to Profit* and to my delight, walked me through their W.R.I.T.E.R. process to make it both readable and marketable, while staying true to the content and to my core voice. The combination of Lucy's attention to detail, and Joe's flair for design led to the publication of a book that I am very proud of and, more importantly, that is fulfilling its purpose – to attract customers pre-sold on my expertise and experience."

Marianne Page, Founder and Director of Bright7, author of
Process to Profit

"This book will prove invaluable to anyone aiming to write a book. Lucy's experienced guidance, and honest feedback helped me to produce a far better book than the one I initially set out to write. Once she liked my draft manuscript, I knew I was on the right track, and was able to quickly finalise my book."

Shireen Smith, IP lawyer, and Founder of Azrights, author,
Legally Branded

"They say everyone has a book in them, if only they could find the time to sit down and write it. Having recently published *Leading with Gravitas: unlock the six keys to impact and influence*, I appreciate the challenges faced by prospective authors looking to publish a book on top of the day job. In *How to Write a Book without the Fuss*, Lucy McCarraher and Joe Gregory take you by the hand and lead you through all the steps you need to take, from nailing your initial concept to going to print. Packed with no-nonsense tips and techniques, it includes advice from published authors to save you reinventing the wheel and keep you inspired along the way. If you're serious about getting your book into the world and sharing your business or self-help message, this is the book for you."

Antoinette Dale Henderson, coach, speaker and author of
Leading with Gravitas: unlock the six keys to impact and influence
www.zomicommunications.co.uk

"I always knew that I wanted to write a book but was daunted at the task of planning it, writing it, and finally would anyone actually read it? With Lucy's coaching everything just seemed to fall into place. She helped me formulate my ideas into a well organised synopsis before embarking on the writing challenge. Her sound publishing and editing background meant my final manuscript was succinct and punchy. Combine that with Joe's extraordinary business background, which was invaluable in my final cover design and content. *How to Write Your Book Without The Fuss* definitely works; I am now published and immensely proud of what Lucy and Joe have helped me to create."

Robin Waite, author of #1 Best Seller, *Online Business Startup*

"Lucy and Joe came along at exactly the time I needed some 'no fuss' guidance – it was as if the Universe had seen me drowning in a sea of unedited manuscript and self-doubt, and thrown me a lifejacket in the guise of Rethink Press. If it hadn't have been for their Attention, Understanding, Trust and Help, my book *Mend the Gap* wouldn't be getting the credible Reaction it is today. Lucy and Joe helped me to believe I had an Original idea, and without their expertise and incredible A.U.T.H.O.R. approach, I wouldn't be the author I am now! Their showing up in my life at that moment was real life magic, and for all they did I am hugely grateful."

Katie Mottram, author of *Mend the Gap;*
A transformative journey from deep despair to spiritual awakening

"Before reading Lucy and Joe's book, I thought I knew what my approach would be. Their absolute clarity about the process of writing a book had be rethinking before the end of the chapter. This is a fantastic guide for the beginner or seasoned writer; it has helped me take a much more detailed and professional approach to writing my first book. This is a really insightful, easy to understand guide to all aspects of writing a self-help book. I have completely changed the structure of my book and know it will be a much better book for Lucy and Joe's help."

Jenny Andersson, CEO JenAndersson Ltd

"Do you want to know the smart and savvy way to write a book which establishes you as an expert and attracts income? Look no further. This content rich book is truly *the* definitive guide."

Sharon Eden, The Depression Coach, MA, Regd MBACP (Accred), author of *Bounce Back from Depression – The No Nonsense Guide to Recovery*
www.bouncebackuk.com

"When I decided to write my book, I was excited about what was ahead of me when I became a published author. I also felt overwhelmed with all the stuff I needed to learn in order to plan, write, and publish something people would talk about. I achieved just that by applying the tips and principles from this great little book."

Michael Serwa, Life Coach and Author of *From Good To Amazing*

CONTENTS

FOREWORD

In any industry you will find Key People of Influence (KPIs). These authorities are the most well-known and highly valued people in their fields.

Their names come up in conversation for all the right reasons. They attract the best opportunities. They earn more money than most and they have more fun.

While their competitors are busy chasing clients, partners and opportunities, Key People of Influence get to pick and choose.

Some people think it takes decades to join this inner circle. They believe authority only comes with degrees, MBAs or doctorates. That influence depends on having a wealthy family or that you need money to make money.

However, there are just five proven steps anyone can take to become a Key Person of Influence within a year. Writing a good book and getting it published is one of them.

In 2010, my first book, *Become a Key Person of Influence*, was published and since that time I've seen first-hand what a vital tool it is. Being the author of a good book is the best way I've found to effortlessly demonstrate your value, attract more interest, increase your influence and raise your income. In fact, that first book had such a huge impact on my business that I've since written two more, which were snapped up and published by Wiley.

Having tested and proven the 5-step Key Person of Influence process across fifty industries, in over a dozen countries, working with over a thousand entrepreneurs, we've also found that over a third of our clients who publish a book double their income in under two years.

While the barriers to entry for writing and publishing a book are now lower than ever, the barriers to excellence have never been higher. There are more books competing for your market's attention, people can share their review with the world in an instant, and retailers are continuing to innovate to weed out the good content from the bad.

So, if you intend to write a book to raise your authority and get your message out to your audience in a big way, you owe it to yourself to write a brilliant book and that's why I urge you to read *How To Write Your Book Without The Fuss*.

I invited Lucy McCarraher to be the KPI Publish Mentor in 2013 because she and her business partner Joe Gregory absolutely get the point of writing and publishing books for entrepreneurs. In fact, since 2003 they've published over 300 titles by expert entrepreneurs with a message and helped many more to craft and write a book that brings business.

If you want to write a book that will have a truly huge impact on your business, Lucy and Joe have absolutely nailed it. From packaging and structuring through to getting it written quickly, easily and well, the advice in this book will give you an edge on your journey to becoming a Key Person of Influence.

Daniel Priestley,
Bestselling author, entrepreneur and creator of
The Key Person of Influence Programme, www.entrevo.com

INTRODUCTION

If you want to write a business or self-help book, get it published and use it as a tool to dramatically raise your profile, the time has never been better. If you want to do all this without the fuss, it makes sense to learn from people who have already done just that. Between us we have written ten self-help books and, through our Bookshaker and Rethink Press publishing houses, have published a further 300 written by other authors.

Lucy is an author, editor, writing coach and publisher, who started her first publishing company while she was still at university. Joe is a graphic designer, author and marketer who turned to publishing full-time in 2003 when he sold thousands of copies of his first self-published book (on marketing). We share a strong track record of success, have a good knowledge of and experience in the current writing and publishing industry, and a clear-eyed approach to the constantly-evolving market of business and self-help books.

What is a self-help book?

Self-help is a broad category, and includes many subject areas, from business, marketing and DIY, to learning plumbing or a new language, coping with relationship problems or bankruptcy, training your brain or acquiring spiritual enlightenment, and everything in between and further afield.

Our definition of a self-help book is:

A book that helps another person improve any aspect of their working or personal life, including business, relationships, emotional management, physical and mental health, spiritual life, finances or any skills. A good self-help book is one that addresses a real problem and provides a genuine solution for the reader that is not easily accessible elsewhere.

'How many a man has dated a new era in his life from the reading of a book.'
HENRY DAVID THOREAU

By the time you've read this self-help book for business and self-help authors, you're going to know:

How to create a winning book idea

Without question, a great book idea is the best starting point for business or self-help authors, but a good idea alone won't get you very far. By the time you've finished reading you should be able to answer 'yes' to the following:

- Do you know if your book idea is really that good?
- Can you summarise your book well in a single sentence?
- Do you know how your book is positioned?
- Does your book have a killer title?

How to find your book's market

The business and self-help markets are massive and varied, but very few authors can claim that their books sell to anyone and everyone looking for improvements in their life. The best way to get your message out there, sell a good number of books and get yourself known as an expert in your field, is to find the niche readers who want and need your message. We want to make sure you have a positive answer to these questions:

- Are you confident your great idea has a commercial (within your niche market) future?
- Can you really say who your book is for without resorting to 'anyone and everyone'?
- Will your book appeal to the people who need and want it, and do you know how to find them?
- Can you easily give strong reasons why prospective readers should buy your book?

How to write your book quickly and easily

We don't subscribe to the belief that anyone can write a useful, well-written and professionally constructed book in a weekend, or even a week – although if you have the material at your fingertips, a fortnight isn't impossible. A robust structure and detailed chapter breakdown of your business or self-help book will, however, make the actual writing a much quicker and easier task. So, once you've got your great idea defined and you know who you're writing for, we'll ensure that you:

- Know the essential elements you need in your business or self-help book
- Can rapidly and easily map out your book before writing a single word
- Have a useful chapter-by-chapter framework to help your book write itself
- Understand the key points of good, grammatical writing and punctuation
- Have immunised yourself against writer's block

How to edit your book to professional standards

Although we would strongly advise any business or self-help author to have their manuscript edited by a professional before it goes to print, we believe that understanding the editing process and rigorously reviewing your own work is the way to make it outstanding.

Testing a draft manuscript with others is also a crucial element in creating an excellent business or self-book, and one which brings you supporters when it comes to marketing and promoting your book.

How to get your book published

Making the right decision here is crucial. Even if you think your goal is to get a contract from a mainstream publisher, or that self-publishing is the only way you'll hang on to all the money from the sales of your book, you need to know all your options and the up-sides and down-sides of each one. Once you've compared the different ways to get your book in print, you will understand:

- The different publishing models and how to work out which one is the right choice for you
- How to format your manuscript professionally
- How to pitch your book idea so that it attracts the kind of publisher or agent you want
- That choosing the right publishing approach will maximise profit from your intellectual property

But first, let's get your objectives for writing a business or self-help book clear.

Planning Your Book

CREATING YOUR WINNING BOOK IDEA

The first step in your journey to writing your business or self-help book is to develop a winning idea that will be worth all the work you are going to put into this project. In this section we will be making sure you know what outcomes you want to achieve, before we help you develop your best idea for your book. We will be helping you to think creatively, but practically, and introducing you to our A.U.T.H.O.R. model of planning your book.

By the time you have worked through this section, you should have one, or maybe several options, for a killer title and subtitle. You will also be clear on your book's niche market, or if not you will have all the tools to research it in more detail.

Before we start looking at how you can write your business or self-help book, we should first ask *why* you want to write it. Writing a book isn't for everyone: even if you have a compelling message and in depth expertise in your area, it may not be best framed within the covers of a book. It's also worth asking whether there is a readership for a book on your subject, or if you will find your audience more easily through blog posts, podcasts, speaking, coaching or other media.

'Writing is hard work, not magic. It begins with deciding why you are writing and whom you are writing for. What is your intent? What do you want the reader to get out of it? What do you want to get out of it? It's also about making a serious time commitment and getting the project done.'

SUZE ORMAN

Why Write A Self-Help Book?

Different authors experience different triggers for writing their book. These typical reasons might resonate with you in deciding whether now is the right time for you to produce your business or self-help book.

What's out there isn't good enough

Lucy was planning to write a fourth novel on the theme of women who were using different types of self-help books to improve their lives. While researching her story, she read a massive range of 'happiness' manuals and became increasingly frustrated with what was available. On the one hand, good content was often buried within convoluted writing and psychological jargon; on the other hand, seekers after a better life were being taken in by mumbo-jumbo and delusional ideas, some of which were downright dangerous. Lucy decided she had to write her own self-help book and partnered with social psychologist Annabel Shaw to bring both simplicity and scientifically supported self-help to an audience she believed was out there.

Debbie Jenkins, who co-authored *The Gorillas Want Bananas* with Joe, said, 'I'm on a mission… I want to change the face of marketing and make the tools that have been shrouded in mystery and hype available to the people who are going to do something with them.'

If you are on a mission to tell the world something important, it's time to write a book.

You have something unique to say

Over the time you have been practising your skills, running your business, consulting to other organisations or coaching individuals, have you discovered a different way of doing things? Do you have an unusual take on your niche subject or do you strongly disagree with the consensus of opinion that's currently in the market place?

There are endless self-help books in the health and fitness market, but personal trainers Tim Drummond and Phil Hawksworth felt they had something very different to say to a niche market of younger women, which went against the grain of some current views, especially in relation to diet. They put together *The 30/30 Body Blueprint* and attracted a lot of media attention with their fresh take on getting and staying fit as part of a busy lifestyle.

'I had wanted to write a book for a while, and there was no time like the present,' said Phil. 'I knew I had a lot of knowledge and experience that would be valuable to the readers so felt that I should put it out there.'

If you have a unique idea or take on solving a very real problem then writing a book will enable you to stake a claim to this unique information and even protect your intellectual property. A published book is a very tangible piece of evidence that you said what you're saying first.

You have an archive of material that is going to waste

For some people, writing up their experience and advice to others is a way of life, whether this is through keeping a regular blog, writing things for other people or just keeping notes or a personal journal. Have you recently realised that you have about enough written material to fill a book and that's exactly what you plan to do with it?

Judy Barber had been collecting her raw food recipes in a scruffy notebook and friends and family were really enjoying the food. For her, putting the information into book form was the logical next step.

'For it to be a really useful self-help book I also wrote sections on the reasons for eating plenty of raw food, on the ingredients and equipment. *Good Raw Food Recipes* put the basics of what I teach into book form so that I have something to share at talks and workshops and in bookshops.'

Being a published author will give you expert status and credibility

If you are an entrepreneur, consultant, coach, small business owner or sole trader, being the author of a book on your niche subject will give you a perceived level of expertise that nothing else can match. Publishing a business or self-help book is now considered a crucial part of the small business platform – much like having a website used to be.

"Writing a book is a tremendous experience. It pays off intellectually. It clarifies your thinking. It builds credibility. It is a living engine of marketing and idea spreading, working every day to deliver your message with authority. You should write one."

SETH GODIN

Louise Walker had worked in many businesses over the past 20 years, holding senior corporate roles in several different disciplines before becoming a marketing director in an international events company. In 2004, Louise formed her own marketing services company and specialises in working with CEOs and business owners in the B2B services sector. Not long ago, wanting to increase her own profile and that of her business, she went on the Key Person of Influence (KPI) programme. There, she was taken through the five KPI steps, of which the second is 'Publish'.

'I didn't want to write a book,' Louise said. 'I wrote it because I could see the value in being a published author, as part of the KPI programme. I remember sitting next to a lady on the Publish Day of the programme and we had to tell each other why we were writing our books. She waxed lyrical about wanting to write several books and was really enthusiastic. When it was my turn I explained my rather less "spiritual" reasons for writing the book: profile and credibility – being recognised as a leader in my field and gaining more business as a result. I don't think she was impressed. Funnily enough she still hasn't finished her book... '

When *From The Ground Up* was published, Louise found that 'People are genuinely impressed when they know that you have written and published a book. Your IP (intellectual property) is being given to lots of people who will hopefully gain some benefit from it for their business. If a reader gains even one piece of advice that helps them to increase their sales or improve what they are doing it really makes you feel that the effort was worthwhile.'

Books bring business

Entrepreneurs and small business owners gain in three key areas when they write and publish a professional business or self-help book. These can be summarised as income, interest and influence.

Income

By far the greatest financial benefit to entrepreneur authors is the high level clients and contracts their books attract.

Marianne Page, Director of Bright7, wrote a book called *Process To Profit* outlining her approach to systemising businesses for the benefit of owner entrepreneurs. In the last six months alone, she gained over £50,000 worth of contracts through three people who read her book: a business owner who had picked it up on holiday and got in touch on his return, anxious to work with her; an old friend who heard she had written a book so read it – and realised how much she could help him; and a franchisee who was recommended it and realised Marianne's system was just what he needed.

She is just one of many small business owners whose books have attracted business, whose prospects come "pre-sold" on their ideas, and want to pay high fees for implementation of a strategy they have already understood and appreciated.

Interest

Many small businesses find it hard to make the transition from working with a select group of clients who know and like them, to being sought after by a wider following. When an entrepreneur crafts their knowledge and processes into book form, they reach an audience they would never have the time or opportunity to contact personally. Their book becomes their ambassador, working 24/7 to spread their name and expertise. When someone googles their subject, name or business, it appears on one of the world's most powerful search engines – Amazon. Not just anyone gets their name on Amazon, only those who have actually taken the time and effort to write a book.

Michael Serwa, a life coach, wrote *From Good To Amazing – no bullshit tips for the life you always wanted,* specifically to raise his profile with the media as well as potential clients. The book has found its way round the world and into the hands of readers who have become fans. Michael and his tips have been featured in popular magazines and newspapers, and he now has his own YouTube channel where he interviews other high profile coaches in his exclusive Mayfair apartment. 'It's all about the book,' in his opinion.

Jacqueline Biggs' *Marketing To Win* shows small businesses how to leverage the marketing strategies of big companies. Once we published her book, she used her own marketing expertise to get her book to a #1 Amazon ranking. We also entered it for the Chartered Management Institute's Book Awards and it was nominated for Best Commuter Read – alongside Sheryl Sandberg's *Lean In* and Daniel Priestley's *Entrepreneur Revolution.* When Jacqueline approached UK government small business support services, it was her book that impressed them and led to her now constant flow of funded SME marketing clients

Influence

There is nothing like having authored a book to accentuate your credentials as a thought leader and authority in your market. Have you noticed how most media 'experts' are authors; how speakers and guests at events have at least one book to their name; how leaders in your industry are likely to have put their ideas into book form?

Adam Hamadache, a consultant in the hotel industry, wrote *Give Your Guest A WOW!* and his ideas on customer service were so far-sighted and widely applicable that his book has sold consistently well within and without his niche market. It has brought him business, raised his profile, and made him a youthful but respected influencer in his industry. Because of his book, Adam is regularly flown to give £1000+ speaking gigs at top hotel industry events at home and abroad, where he gets to tell established KPIs how to up their customer service game. And they take it from him – because he is the author of an excellent and professional book.

Being a best-selling author and making loads of money

You'll have noticed we've left this one until last. This is because no matter how brilliant your idea for a business or self-help book, no matter how many people will benefit greatly from reading your message – if your reason for writing is simply, or even mainly, to make money from book sales, you may want to find another driver for your decision. Many authors of business or self-help books have poured time, energy, and passion into crafting their experiences and expertise into books, and only a very few of them have been able to live off the proceeds of their book alone.

Writing a business or self-help book will bring you satisfaction, self-development, respect, business and added value in all manner of ways, but if it's all about the royalty money for you, this may not be the right project.

Whatever combination of reasons you've identified from those we've mentioned, or others we haven't, they will influence what ingredients you bring to creating a winning business or self-help book.

THE A.U.T.H.O.R. MODEL

A	U	T	H	O	R
ATTENTION	UNDERSTAND	TRUST	HELP	ORIGINAL	REACTION

When we coach individual authors or mentor groups through writing their business or self-help book, we use our A.U.T.H.O.R. model to help new authors focus on the most important aspects of their book. A.U.T.H.O.R. stands for:

A – Attention. How are you going to attract attention to your book, from your market, your readers and your industry? This is important when you work on defining your winning idea and creating a killer title and subtitle. Bear this in mind throughout the preparation and writing of your book, but we will be working on this particularly in this first section of the book.

U – Understand. In order to write a business or self-help book, you must know well and empathise with the problems faced by your market, and the central questions that your potential readers are asking and demanding an answer to. If you can provide the solutions and answers in your book you have a captive audience, so getting clarity on this understanding is an essential first step. Using our checklists and processes in this section will help you analyse your understanding.

T – Trust. Your readers must believe that you have the authority and credibility to offer solutions that they can trust in. Your personal/professional story is a vital element in creating this trust, as are your credentials, qualifications, experience and proof of having delivered answers and solutions already. We provide you with methods to incorporate your trustworthiness while preparing and writing your business or self-help book

H – Help. This refers to the main body of your book – how you are able to help your readers solve their problems and answer their questions. Your book is their Help, and its clear structure, well-developed content, logical and tested process is how they will get this from you. Everything in sections two and three is focused on helping you deliver the best possible help to your readers.

O – Original. However great your material and method may be, if it's the same as many others out there, your book will not stand out or show you to be an outstanding thought leader or authority in your field. We will be helping you to evaluate and refine what constitute the original elements of your content.

R – Reaction. When you are planning your book, writing your book, building pre-publication buzz for your book; when you are getting your book published, selling your published book, getting feedback from readers and wanting them to take action as a result of your book, you are looking for a strong reaction. Following the steps we take you through in this book will ensure that you get the reaction you want from writing your business and self-help book all the way along.

Defining Your Winning Idea

Are you one of those lucky people who wake up with a new idea for a book every morning? If so, you can use the checklists, tools and self-tests in this section to review your ideas and pick the one most likely to connect with your perfect audience. See it as a process of elimination rather than creation.

If, however, like many people you struggle to come up with new ideas, or you have a good idea but don't know how to make it outstanding, this section of the book will be crucial. We're going to show you ways to generate plenty of new ideas, how to position your idea to be unique, test it to find ways to improve it, and then come up with a winning title.

First, let's talk a little about getting into the right state of mind.

The Creative State

Being creative is not something that only the inspired or artistic can achieve. It's a skill and a process, and, like everything else we do well, it can be learned and developed. If you think creativity is not something that comes naturally to you (although it probably does in areas other than writing), or it's not something you've had a lot of practice at, you'll be relieved to know it's not a magical ability and there are defined steps to follow.

There are three elements in coming up with the right idea and they involve different types of brain activity. Without knowing this, it's easy to get derailed by trying to do them all at once. To avoid brain freeze, take these steps one at a time.

1. Generating Ideas

- Any and every idea has potential.
- Don't self-edit or criticise; simply record all the ideas you come up with.
- Use word association, brainstorming, mind-mapping or any other method of generating and recording ideas that works for you. Try all of them.

2. Reviewing Ideas

- Now is the time to allow your inner critic its say.
- Typically this will involve a process of elimination.
- Sort ideas onto a Keep or Kill scale:

KEEP | | | | | | | KILL

Record the outcomes of the reviewing stage.

3. Improving/Testing Ideas

- Choose your top five ideas and see how you can build on them.
- Refine your ideas further until you have three solid concepts, from which to select.
- Write them on a single sheet of paper and leave for up to 24 hours.
- Come back to the list and see which one jumps out at you.
- Add further meat to the bare bones until you've got a first-draft book proposal planned out.

EIGHT TIPS FOR GETTING INTO A MORE CREATIVE STATE OF MIND

1. Get yourself somewhere comfortable and clear from clutter and other demands (work, phone, internet etc).
2. Clear your mind with whatever works for you. Listening to or playing music, going for a walk, exercise, drawing or painting or having a long bath works for many. If you're into meditation or yoga, use that.

---

3 Silence your inner critic: that voice in your head that edits stuff before it comes out of your mouth. It's often useful, but it can stifle creativity. First, accept that it is useful in some contexts and then decide to give this critical voice a little break.

4 Pose creative questions, using words like, 'How can I...?', 'What if...?', 'What's interesting about...?'

5 Dwell on an idea. If you have a skill, a theme or an over-riding feeling about what you want to create, meditate upon it. Simply let it expand to fill your mind and let the connections in your brain start firing.

6 Take a notebook to bed. Do some free writing about any ideas you've come up with just before you go to sleep and as soon as you wake up in the morning. If you wake up in the night with an insight, you'll be able to note it down (although it may seem less brilliant in the morning).

7 Remind yourself that you use your creativity to solve problems and explain things to others every single day. If you've been told you're not creative and you've believed it in the past, it's time to put aside this old and inaccurate belief.

8 Remember times when you've been at your most creative. Rekindle those feelings, consciously in the here and now. Creativity is like a muscle – it grows with use.

Does your book idea have legs?

The big idea is the driving force behind the rest of your book. If you are going to be writing about your area of business expertise, this idea may be your 'pitch', as defined by Daniel Priestley in his book, *Become A Key Person of Influence*.

> *'A pitch is a powerful set of words that you send out to the world again and again. Eventually, if you stick at it and really get the pitch perfect, you will get what you pitch for. In business, if you get it right you can raise money, attract a team, engage partners and inspire clients to take you on. If you are a change maker, you will eventually attract a following, upset the status quo and see a shift in your cause.'*

If you can refine your book idea, like your pitch, to one or two succinct, telling and selling sentences, it is the foundation for everything that follows. Get it right and your book will almost write itself, people will talk about it, the packaging will be strong, the marketing will seem effortless and the media will love you. Get it wrong and the writing process will be tough, people won't notice it, the packaging will be bland, the marketing will seem impossible and the media will ignore you.

Score your book on the following components as follows:
0 = disagree totally, 1 = agree slightly, 2 = agree totally

My Book...

☐ Makes a big promise that's attractive to readers

☐ Answers one of life's big questions

☐ Solves something no other book has solved

☐ Stands strongly for a particular thing, idea or belief

☐ Stands strongly against a particular thing, idea or belief

☐ Fits well within a universally popular interest or trend

☐ Is considered unique, cool, outrageous, contentious or dangerous

☐ Fits a niche market that you can clearly identify

☐ Provides timeless wisdom/principles that won't go out of date in the near future

☐ Provides hard-to-find, how-to information on a particular subject

☐ Is written by a 'go to expert' on the subject

☐ Is the first or best on a hot new topic or trend

☐ Makes people say, 'You've just got to read this'

☐ Is packed with sound-bites that people can share and quote easily

☐ Can be summed up effectively in one sentence

Your Score

0 – 3: Back to the drawing board. This isn't a good idea yet and if you go ahead without trying to improve it, you're going to have to work hard to make it sell. Ask yourself, 'How can I make this idea tick more boxes?' If you're not sure, keep reading for tips and tools to help you.

3 – 6: Room for improvement. Your book, with the right promotion, will probably do okay, but isn't it worth making the idea better before you go through all the hard work to come? Ask yourself, 'How can I make this idea tick more boxes?' Keep reading to learn some tricks.

6 – 10: We would publish it. Your book idea is truly a thing of beauty. But the idea is just the first step on a long publishing journey. You'll need to execute the writing, packaging and marketing impeccably to really benefit from your idea's full potential.

15: You cheated. Some of the components of a winning book idea conflict with others, so, please re-do the test and actually read and think this time. However, if you still score 15, we'd like to hear your idea. Contact us at lucy@rethinkpress.com

What is your book's positioning strategy?

Although positioning is often seen as a marketing task, your book's position must be clear right from the outset because it has a profound effect on how the book is written, how it is packaged, how it is marketed and much more.

A lot of over-complicated nonsense has been written on positioning – and some people waste a small fortune on it – but it really just boils down to this:

'To survive, each [book] must be perceptibly distinct from all the others. There are three ways to narrow the competitive field: Narrow the benefit Narrow the method of delivering it Narrow the audience'

CATHERINE MACCOUN

To narrow the 'benefit' of your book, and the 'audience' for it, ask yourself what does it stand for? You should be able to say categorically that your book stands either *for* something or *against* something. If you sit in the middle your book will stand for nothing and will appeal to nobody.

Use the following simple scale to determine your book's for/against position. The more extreme the better. If you're in the middle, you'll get lost amongst all the other 'me-too' stuff on your subject. It's much better to have an excited niche audience than an uninterested mainstream.

AGAINST | | | | | | | FOR

Later we will also be looking at positioning your book in relation to the competition.

To narrow the 'method of delivering' your book, you can look at different options for publishing, which we explore later; and you can consider which formats, or combination of formats, will best deliver your message to your intended audience, from PDF download, e-book, paperback or hardback.

Positioning your book by 'chunking'

If the above positioning strategy seems too simplistic for you and you'd rather get to grips with your book's positioning in more detail to ensure you've missed nothing out, here is a powerful tool.

There are three main ways we sort data in our minds. They are:

1. **Chunking Up** – where you summarise all the benefits/problems and reasons why/why not
2. **Chunking Down** – where you tease out all the detail of what something is or is not
3. **Chunking Laterally** – using metaphors, analogies and examples of what a thing is like or is unlike

Here's how to use the concept of Chunking as a practical tool to position your book idea:

1. On a big sheet of paper draw your own matrix, copying the image on the next page.
2. Write a theme, topic, audience, main idea or your subject in the centre (draw it as a picture too if you like).
3. Use the questions in the image to help you chunk in all the directions (up, down, laterally); and *against* (left) and *for* (right) from the main theme.
4. Ideally, write all your ideas on post-it notes so you can easily sort them and move them around to help find your position.

5. Use this information to clearly state…
   * What your book *is not* or does not stand for.
   * What your book *is* or does stand for.
   * What your book *won't* give readers.
   * What your book *will* give readers.
   * What subjects your book *won't* cover.
   * What subjects your book *will* cover.
   * Who your book *is not* for.
   * Who your book *is* for.

These last two will help you to further narrow and define the audience for your book. Although it may seem counter-intuitive to think about reducing your potential readership, your book will only succeed if it addresses the niche market, to which your experience and expertise brings value.

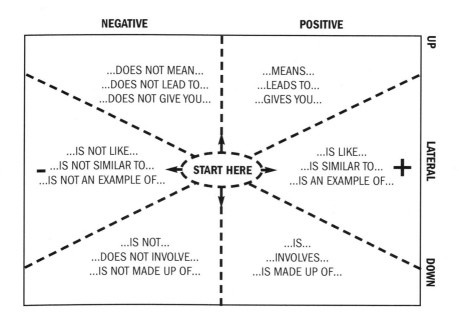

Creating your book title and subtitle

Your book's title and subtitle are probably the most important things to consider at the initial ideas stage. Some publishers may want to change it, but your title (even when pitching to publishers) says a lot about you, your position and your book's chances. Never underestimate the power of a good title.

Here are eight things to consider while creating your winning book title:

1. A good title is like a good headline, so model newspapers and magazines
2. Your title's number one job is to make people want to open the book
3. Make your title dramatic and use powerful, active and emotive words
4. Make a big promise or say something shocking or provocative
5. Ask a leading question to make prospective readers curious
6. Pose a conundrum that will engage your audience
7. If you have a clever, witty or one-word main title then be sure your sub-title explains your book's big promise
8. Don't try to be clever if a more obvious title is stronger

Louise Walker chose *From The Ground Up* as the title of her book on marketing by going through a rigorous process:

'Choosing the title was quite a long process – I had a brainstorm session and just dumped everything I could think of onto paper. I followed the guidance of keeping it short and punchy, went through all of the titles I had thought of and sense-checked that they applied to my book – I wanted something that had a relevance to the content.

'I narrowed the title choices down and then got some feedback from clients and peers. I also looked at other books in the same sector of the marketplace to check that the title had not been used and also to see what others were using.

'I made the final decision based on these criteria and then wrote the sub-heading – *Making marketing work throughout your business* – to give a brief overview of the subject matter in the book.'

Judy Barber, for a very different kind of business or self-help book, looked at each word in detail for the title and subtitle of her raw food recipes:

'*Good Raw Food Recipes* popped up in a mastermind group and is perfect because it's easy for people to find on search engines. It fits with the title of my first book, *Good Question! The Art of Asking Questions to Bring About Positive Change*. The subtitle, *Delicious Raw and Living Food for Energy and Wellness* starts with the word "Delicious" to engage taste buds. "Raw and Living" engages those already in the know as well as those discovering an interest. "Energy and Wellness" tell the benefits and position me within my niche by declaring my focus.'

Twenty words that add power to any book title

1. How To
2. Secrets of
3. Stop
4. Start
5. Discover
6. Unleash
7. Change
8. Never
9. Always
10. Overcome

11. Unlock
12. Beat
13. Free
14. You, Your
15. Ways To
16. The Key To
17. The Secret To
18. Master
19. Become
20. Learn to

Have you come up with your book's killer title?

Score your title on the following components:

0 = disagree totally, 1 = agree slightly, 2 = agree totally

My book's title...

☐ Makes a big promise

☐ Poses a question

☐ Says something contentious, shocking or risky

☐ Creates curiosity

☐ Is easy to remember and share

☐ Is unique and catchy

☐ Clearly indicates what the book is about

☐ Would work well as a headline in a newspaper or sales letter

☐ Is easy to spell and pronounce

☐ Uses simple, dramatic and/or sensational words

Your Score

0-3: Do not put it on your book. This headline will put people to sleep, won't grab attention and will possibly spell instant failure for your book's chances. Ask yourself, 'How can I make my title tick more boxes?' It's really worth getting this as good as you can.

4-6: Could be a winner. It really depends *where* you scored highly. If you strongly agreed with just *one* of the first three components of a good book title then it's probably a great title. If you didn't, ask yourself, 'How can I make this title tick one of the first three boxes?'

7+: You have a killer title. This will be a huge asset to your book and, as you'll see, will add powerful impact to your position as an authority. The title alone will significantly influence a publisher's decision to publish, or a reader's decision to buy your book.

Mark Tier's *Becoming Rich,* published 2005 in hardcover by St Martin's Press, New York, had several tens of thousands of dollars spent on publicity – and died. Around the same time, Mark's own company, Inverse Books (Hong Kong)'s edition of *The Winning Investment Habits of Warren Buffett & George Soros,* published in 2004, completely sold out its first hardcover print run and went for a second print run. Same book; different title.

To put this in perspective, his own edition was only on sale in a few countries: Australia, New Zealand, Hong Kong, Singapore, Malaysia, and a few smaller Asian markets. St Martin's Press, however, had the whole of the US, Canada, and the Philippines to itself, plus most of the rest of the world (excluding the British Commonwealth) on a non-exclusive basis.

Mark Tier sold *twice* as many copies of the same book in a market less than one-tenth the size of St Martins'. On a simple *per capita* projection, St Martin's Press could have sold some 100,000+ copies of *Winning Investment Habits* instead of 4,650 copies of *Becoming Rich.*

Luckily, when it came time for the paperback edition, Mark convinced the publisher to use his original title.

Read the full story here:
http://marktier.com/eclecticinvestor/marketing/double-or-triple-your-book%E2%80%99s-sales-by-rewriting-just-5-to-10-words.html#!

This story again illustrates why it's important to chunk down into detail in order to connect with your readers. The first title was too generic, bland and could appeal to anybody. The better-selling title focused in on the process (investing) and the source of inspiration (Buffet and Soros). It goes without saying that people will have strong views on these two financiers (not all people will like their approach even if they can acknowledge their success), but it enabled the author to clearly connect with his target market.

With a winning idea and a killer title and subtitle, you can move on to defining the market for your business or self-help book.

Finding Your Book's Market

Having a winning idea is a great start, but if your book's subject is so obscure that it has no appeal for more than a handful of readers, is all the effort you will put into writing it worth your while? This step will ensure you have identified and can access a solid market for your book, which can make the difference between success and failure.

To understand what your readers are looking for, and what you with your expertise can offer them, try answering the following questions: What are your market's biggest problems? What stresses, strains and pains do your clients experience? What keeps them up at night? What questions do they regularly ask you? What will happen if their problem persists?

If your book is going to provide a solution to these problems, or answers to your market's questions, you should be onto a winning idea.

Does your book have a future?

You should be able to tick every single box in this list.

☐ My book solves a problem or addresses a need my market actually has

☐ The market isn't saturated with lots of books that already promise what my book promises and in exactly the same way

☐ The people in my market actually buy and read books

☐ There are already other books that hit a similar market to mine and are selling well

☐ There are definitely people who want it and/or need it

☐ It solves a current problem or facilitates an achievement

☐ It is unique but still fits neatly into an existing/popular/mature category

Where is your book's niche?

Finding a niche is another topic that is too often presented in an over-complicated way. Quite simply, if your book appeals to 'anyone and everyone', you don't have a niche.

'A fresh approach is critical for success in our changing economy. Small business owners miss out too easily on the opportunities that are available to them because they have not clearly defined their niche.'

RACHEL HENKE, *THE NICHE EXPERT*

If your book *does* happen to appeal to 'everyone and anyone', don't worry. Make it for 'someone' anyway. You could either produce lots of different versions of the book for different niches, or plan ahead to ensure you find the top three niches and focus on selling and marketing to those first. The worst thing you can do is try to sell to everyone at once because your efforts will be scattered and your effectiveness diluted.

There are two ways to choose a niche:

1. **Topic**: The focus of a topically targeted book will be an interest, skill, goal, hobby, sport or specific subject and could potentially attract someone interested in *that* topic. This can be defined more simply as 'What is the book about?'

2. **Demographic:** The focus of a demographically targeted book will be the experience, age, gender, lifestyle, social group, sexual preference, location, religion, nationality, ethnicity, income, profession, rank, education, etc of your target market. By its nature, it forces you to generalise about a section of the population so you can make your message resonate with them. This can be defined more simply as 'Who is the book for?'

It's possible to niche a business or self-help book solely on topic, but you add extra power to your book's proposition if you also identify (and target) a specific demographic too.

When you're writing a business or self-help book the topic is usually obvious and limited to a few options (based on the subject you've identified and your own expertise), but the demographic variations can be huge. Use the following approach to map out your potential targets.

1. Draw a matrix with the various key topics (What) of your book across the top (columns) and the various demographic variables (Who) down the side (rows).

2. If you're having trouble coming up with demographic groups, think about yourself first. Do you run your own business? Are you employed in someone else's business? Do you manage other people? Do you want to run your own business? How old are you? Are you a baby-boomer? How much do you earn? Are you single? Are you a parent? What do you do in your spare time? Do you have any spare time? What are your religious beliefs? What are your political beliefs? Once you've defined yourself you'll easily be able to find alternatives for other groups.

3. Anywhere you get an interesting or appealing combination (in that it will create a unique take on a book) of the 'What' and the 'Who', write a potential book description/title. You don't have to find something for them all, as some combinations will clearly show you that those demographic targets just wouldn't be right.

Here's an example of three very different topics to illustrate how this approach works (your own book will ideally have a tighter topic):

	TRAVEL	SELF DEFENCE	BUSINESS
BEGINNER	The First Timer's Skiing Holiday	How Not To Hit Like A Geek – Even If You Are One	The Business Startup Action Plan
ADVANCED	Off The Beaten Track: Adventurous Holiday Ideas	Peak Performance Training Drills For Martial Artists	Time for Growth: Take Your Business To The Next Level
TEACHER	Peak Season Travel: How To Cut The Cost	Teachers: Stay Safe, Stay Legal	Be In Demand As A Home Tutor
ENTREPRENEUR	How To Run Your Business... Anywhere	Bare Knuckle Selling: Knockout Sales Tactics	Win The Dragon: How To Get Funding For Your Great Idea
TEEN	The Travelling Teen:Teen-Friendly Travel Destinations	Beat The Bully: Non-Violent Self Defence That Works	How To Make Money While Your Friends Just Spend
MOTHER	Don't Forget The Kids. How To Enjoy Exotic Holidays With The Kids in Tow	The Way of The Mum: Self Defence To Keep Your Family Safe	The Mumpreneur's Guide To Business Success
STUDENT	Gap Year Traveller: Seeing The World When You're Broke	Stay Safe on Campus: How To Avoid Trouble and Defend Yourself	Student Millionaire: 7 of The Top Internet Businesses Were Started By People Like You.
RETIREE	Top 10 Cruises For The Silver Surfer	Old Dogs Still Bite: Self Defence For The Over 60s	Hobbies That Pay: 101 Ways To Boost Your Retirement Income and Enjoy It

Do you need a demographic niche for your book?

Some people would argue that making a book too demographically focused limits the potential for sales. In some cases this might be true and, if there is no justifiable reason for defining the demographic, don't do it.

If your book has already been written without an obvious 'Who' – don't worry. You can still use this matrix to help you decide on a target(s) for your marketing efforts. Even a generic self-defence book can be made to appeal to a unique demographic if you focus your publicity effort, articles and press releases on that demographic.

To sum this up, if you've niched correctly on both the 'what' and the 'who', your readers will be able to say: *'It's a book on _____ and it's written for people like me.'*

Does your book appeal to your niche market?

If you're still not sure whether you have defined your book's niche, use this simple, but powerful, checklist. If you can tick every box then you will have found a clear market that will love your book.

☐ Your ideal reader is easily identifiable by age, gender, nationality, education-level or other demographic attribute.

☐ Your ideal reader has a very specific interest or need.

☐ Your ideal reader has money and is willing to spend some of it (usually much more than the cost of your book) on fulfilling their need/want.

☐ Your ideal readers spend time with others like them in places that are easy for you to find and access.

☐ You have something that they will really love because it: solves a real problem for them; gives them what they want, better than anyone else is giving it; meets their needs/wants in a unique or exciting way; is new to them.

Now use this simple scale to determine your book's niche-ability. You want to get as close to the left as possible and ensure that the 'someone' you're appealing to is made up of enough individual 'somebodies' to make your niche a profitable one.

SOMEONE ☐☐☐☐☐☐ ANYONE

Quick and easy ways to do book market research

The longer you linger at the research stage the longer it will take for your book to get into the hands of readers. Making sure there's a market is important, but it can be done fast with cost-free and easily available tools.

Tracking market trends

This will give you a really good feel for how popular a particular subject is in relation to other similar topics and whether it's a growth area.

1. Go to *www.google.com/trends*
2. Choose a keyword or phrase related to your book's main theme/topic.

3. Use the dropdowns to select specific geographic regions and timeframes.
4. Separate multiple search terms separated with a comma to compare them directly with one another.

Finding popular blogs and topics

If lots of people are blogging on a subject and many others are interested in their posts, you'll have a great target of well-connected influencers to give review copies of your book to when it comes to promoting it. Tim Ferris, bestselling author of *The 4-Hour Workweek* befriended bloggers and got their support to help make his book a huge success.

1. Go to *www.technorati.com*
2. Click the 'Popular' tag and see what's hot right now.
3. Use the tabs to further search by things like news, movies and books.
4. You can also use the keyword search to find blogs and posts on your topic; to gauge what people are interested in; and the potential for finding connectors when it's time to promote your book.

Gauging your book's market size

Google provides some powerful free tools, one of which is Google Adwords. For more detail than we can go into here, buy and read the most recent edition of *Adwords for Dummies* by Howie Jacobson. In the meantime…

1. Go to *www.google.com/adwords*
2. Sign up as an advertiser (this will come in handy when it's time for promotion anyway).
3. You now have access to tools that will show how many people searched for a particular term, phrase or topic in the last month and how many advertisers are competing for that particular word or phrase.
4. You should have a useful number to make an educated guess on the total market and you'll be able to see whether other people (advertisers) are making an income from serving it.

The greatest book marketing research tool

You probably use this tool every day, but you may not have thought of it as a market research tool until now. Of course, we're talking about Amazon. You can sort by keywords and best-seller lists on specific subjects; you can sort other authors' books by sales rank; you can uncover what's wrong with the competition; and, when you know where to look, you can even make a good guess about how many copies a title is selling.

1. Go to *www.amazon.com* or *www.amazon.co.uk*, depending where your main target market is based.
2. Use Amazon's search bar to look for competitors (it ranks them by most popular by default).
3. Check both print and Kindle versions of the book. It may help you to find out in which format other books in your niche are selling best.

4. Also use the categories section to see what's popular in more general subject areas.
5. Click on books that are doing well for a similar topic/audience to yours.
6. Check the overall Sales Rank of these books. If a book is consistently in the top 2,000 for sales rank for Kindle or print over a week or month then assume it's reaching a strong market.
7. If none of the books catering to your same target/topic are ranked this highly, you've either found an opportunity to provide something really good in this category – or there isn't much of a market and you may need to rethink.

If you find a real star in your area, look at the following things (even buying the book to do this) and be prepared to model elements of your own book on them:

- Check out the cover – what's the big promise? What's the title? Does it look professional or funky? Cluttered or simple? Academic or accessible?
- Check out the blurb – who's the book pitched at? Novice/Advanced?
- Check out the 'Look Inside' and review the Table of Contents, Reviews, Foreword, writing style or any other keys to why the book is doing well.
- Check out the price – is it priced for mass-market appeal or is it priced for high value? Is Amazon offering a discount? A discount by Amazon means the book is selling well and it's worth their while losing a little to promote sales further.

- Is the Kindle version sufficiently cheaper than the print version to attract budget or impulse buyers?

All this competitive research will give you useful data to enable you to differentiate your book, price it correctly (you could average the top ten books on your subject to do this), set your discount and ensure your book isn't missing any tricks.

Summary

Now you've read this chapter, you will have learned about the A.U.T.H.O.R. model and gained clarity around the first two steps: gaining Attention for your book and Understanding your market's central question or problem.

You should be clear about why you want and need to write your business or self-help book; you will have defined your book's winning idea and have a strong working title and subtitle.

You now know how to research your book's niche market and have all the tools if there's more work to do there,

Let's move on to the vital Preparation you must do before you start writing your business or self-help book.

2

PREPARING TO WRITE YOUR BOOK

Now you've got the killer idea, come up with a snappy title and found a niche market for your business or self-help book, it's time to get down to the essential work of planning and structuring. It may well be that your expertise lies predominantly in the subject matter of your book, rather than writing, and that you feel a little daunted by the job that lies ahead. Stick with us. There is almost always a hard way and an easy way to do things, and we're going to show you the easy way to get those words and thoughts out of your head and onto the page. The important thing is to take it step by step – and the first steps are to create a solid structure before you start writing your content.

Here are four steps to planning your book the easy way:

1. Ensure you know your book's overall approach – we'll be looking at typical business or self-help formats to help you decide on yours.
2. Map out your entire book so you can see any gaps in the overall content and make certain you're not missing anything important.
3. Know how many words you're aiming for and work out how many words each chapter should contain, on average, to create the whole book.

4. Make sure your book is professionally topped and tailed with all the additional sections beyond your main content.

The Promise

This is where you move along the A.U.T.H.O.R. from Understanding your market's central question or problem, to building their Trust in you and providing them with the Help they are looking for. These two together constitute your Big Promise.

From the moment they pick it up, or see your book online, your reader should feel excited and eager to invest the next few hours of their life reading it. To make them feel like this, your book has to have a hook; a reason for them to keep reading. How will it do this? By making your readers believe you are going to tell them something important that they don't already know, and that you have the authority and knowledge to do so.

Your book cover – front and back – and the Introduction, which is what people will turn to first, whether they are physically holding it or 'Looking Inside' online, must talk about the benefits to them first, and the features only where necessary. Added to this, your business or self-help book must present you as the expert they need to listen to – and it must have a call to action.

The hook to your reader is your big promise (or promises) to them – which you then have to deliver throughout the book in order to keep your readers reading. If you keep them reading and interested they are more likely to act on your advice, improve the aspect of their life they hoped to, and then begin talking all about your book and its wonderful promise to their friends and colleagues, both in person and on social media.

You can deliver this to them in a numbers of ways.

Four common business or self-help book archetypes

In the realm of business or self-help writing there are some common formats you can use to define the type of book you want to write. The following archetypes give you one more element to clarify before you start planning a structure. As you already know, the less thinking you have to do while you're actually writing, the easier it is to get your book written.

Archetype 1: The Factual 'How To' Book

This type of book usually deals with self-development, business, sports or hobbies where the details are not likely to change very quickly (i.e. they relate to stable subjects and not rapidly advancing trends) and the facts are pretty much widely accepted.

Examples: psychology and relationships, martial arts and athletics, selling and persuasion, motivation and inspiration, spirituality and superstition, business or self-help success and goal achievement, arts and crafts, mainstream (and accepted) science, etc.

Pros:

- Long shelf life (doesn't need constant revisions).
- Solves problems / offers solutions / gives useful information.
- Easy to define target market and identify competitors.

Cons:

- Can be difficult to differentiate your book because the facts are pretty standard and accepted, so you can't write a whole lot of new stuff.
- Competition is often high as older and well-liked books will still be relevant in a mature category.
- Unless you can find a way to present your book in a contentious or other attention-grabbing way you haven't got a very newsworthy book.

Consider:

- Reader sophistication – a book for beginners will be very different to one for experts on many of these subjects. If there is a steep learning curve then it may be better to create a series of books to cover each stage.
- To overcome the differentiation problem, see if you can present the information in a new and exciting way or find one existing paradigm and disagree with it.
- Packaging your book to stand out from the other books in this category.

Archetype 2: The Technical Tutorial Book

This type of business or self-help book typically deals with very specific subjects where the details are important, the facts continue to evolve over time, and often change very quickly, if not constantly. This may apply to very cutting edge subjects and technology, and one of the few areas in which your book could be a 'first'.

Examples: law and medicine, software tutorials, programming, web applications, technology, trends, vehicle repair manuals, social media, government, energy.

Pros:

- If you can build a loyal reader base for this type of book then you can re-sell them the same content (with a few updates) each year without fear of competing with your older and now defunct editions.
- Easy to define your target market and identify competitors.
- You can ride the wave of popularity around a subject or technology (there are many social media books being published currently and some of them will be winners as people are hungry for *any* information they can get their hands on).
- If you already know how to do the thing you're writing a book on then it's easy, you just write it down step-by-step.

Cons:

- Standards, technologies and rules change so the book will go out of date very quickly – the subject could become obsolete in a short time.
- Short shelf-life (needs regular revisions which could mean unsold stock if you have printed or bought copies in advance, and a yearly task to revise the book).
- A high-risk book with a small time-window to make a return and a risk that information could be out of date even by the time it goes to print.
- You're dealing with facts so it may not be the easiest book to inject personality, contentiousness or newsworthiness into, which could give you a harder job with the marketing.
- The subject and not the author is the real star so it may be harder to build back-end kudos for yourself from this kind of book.
- The edit will often require someone with both editing and technical skills related to the subject, increasing the cost and time involved in this phase.

Consider:

- Reader sophistication. If there is a steep learning curve then it may be better to create a series of books to cover each stage.
- Minimising your exposure to risk by looking at producing short e-books and selling them as an updatable series instead.
- If you're an author looking for a mainstream publishing

contract then aim to get this as a one-off-payment commission only. The likelihood you'll make much money in royalties over the long term from this type of book is low, so it's not the best model for building a long term royalty income.

Archetype 3: The 'Feel Good' Inspiration Book

This Archetype comes in a variety of formats, including:

My Story – the author's own experience of (usually) moving from a bad place to a good (often portrayed as great) place, and what they learned on the way that will help you to do the same. Examples: *A Woman's Guide To Forgiving Infidelity* by Christina Young, *Eat, Pray, Love* by Elizabeth Gilbert.

The Metaphor – a story, sometimes with mythic qualities, that takes the reader on a journey through which they learn some truths of life. Examples: *The Alchemist* by Paul Coelho, *Who Moved My Cheese?* by Spencer Johnson.

Journal/Daily Inspiration – a selection of the author's philosophy, wit or wisdom, packaged into, for instance, daily readings, applications to different areas of life, case studies from the author's or other people's lives. Example: *From Good to Amazing* by Michael Serwa, *The Writer's Way* by Julia Cameron.

Books in this genre tend to differ from the previous two in that they give a lot more of the 'what and why' than the 'how'. If you're tempted to write a business or self-help book in this format, make sure it's backed up with solid, usable and practical action and exercises. There are some worryingly misleading, if not downright dangerous, books that fit this archetype, as Lucy and her co-author Annabel Shaw point out in *The Real Secret*.

Pros:

- Giving people inspiration to move out of difficult places, or belief that they can achieve what they want most in the world, draws many willing punters, so you can sell a lot of books if you get the marketing right.
- There's a market in events, seminars, audios and home-study courses in this area, so it's a great way to build a longer-term business based on your book. If you tell a good story about your own experience and this resonates with other people's lives, they will always want to read, hear and buy more.
- Recession proof. When things are bad these books can often sell better as people look for answers and hope. When things are good people aspire to even greater heights and look for quick fixes and easy ways to get more 'good stuff'.
- Often timeless, these kinds of books typically deal with universal 'laws', 'principles', spiritual/emotional attitudes and ancient wisdom, and therefore do not date.
- The media loves this kind of material and its authors, so with the right packaging (for you and your book) you can get lots of coverage and raise your profile.
- If you run a coaching company or host live events then this kind of book will work really well to attract clients.

Cons:

- Be careful about offering unsubstantial and/or unsubstantiated advice to people who really need help. There can be a backlash, from readers and the media.
- Where there's lots of money to be made you'll always find lots of competition. There are a few gurus who really dominate here and, despite their personable and friendly image, they are tough and savvy business people.
- Success with this kind of book is often more of a beauty-pageant than really about the content. If you've got a great face for radio, feel awkward in social situations, are uncharismatic or otherwise not what the media deem celebrity material, you should stick to writing something that can stand on its own merit.

Consider:

- Making sure you back up this kind of book with genuinely useful 'how to' information. There are robust books in this category that provide well-researched and very useful action to go with the inspiration.
- Getting media training and even an image consultant to ensure you're ready to take on the media-friendly gurus and experts already out there.
- Developing your skills as an orator. The best way to make this kind of book sell (and in turn attract business for your high-value coaching and workshops) is to connect directly with your audience.

Archetype 4: The Expert Interviews Book

This kind of book is composed of material drawn from interviews with experts in the subject of your book, usually structured into chapters covering the different areas the author has asked them about. This format of book is entirely dependent on the quality of the interviewees, either in terms of their knowledge or experience, and/or their status as perceived by your market. Here the author acts as more of a curator for good advice. Effective books of this kind have very specific messages at their core and the author/interviewer ensures the questions draw out information that lead to a coherent set of tips or steps for the reader to follow.

Examples: *Secrets of Successful Women Entrepreneurs* and *The Growth Story: Successful Business Growth Strategies used by Women Entrepreneurs* by Sue Stockdale; *Good Question* by Judy Barber.

Pros:

- If you can get them to agree to be interviewed (and many people are likely to be flattered by your interest and the idea of being featured in a book), you get to meet, and develop relationships with, some of your heroes and find out the secrets of their success.
- You get some really strong material from your interviewees with quotable quotes and original content.
- The names of your experts/celebrities will help sell the book.
- Your interviewees may also help you market your book.

- If you have similar experience to your interviewees, you can raise your status through your connection with them.
- You may be able to record the interviews and repurpose these as products in their own right.
- You don't necessarily require any expertise on the subject of your book, though if your aim is to be known as an expert in the field this could be a liability.

Cons:

- You are not the star of your own book as the expertise of the interviewees is what people are buying.
- You will probably not be seen as a thought leader in your own right, through acting in a journalistic role for your interviewees.
- Unless you can ask in-depth and knowledgeable questions, your own expertise in your book's subject is not validated.
- You are not in control of the integrity or public view of your subjects; they may fall out of fashion or from grace with the media, or their views may be discredited.
- Contributors might want a cut of the revenue or a fee upfront.
- Pulling a book of this nature together can feel like herding cats. Interviewees will almost certainly want to see how you've presented the interview and are likely to want some editorial input (their reputation is potentially on the line). If you need approval before you can proceed you may have one contact who holds up the whole publication process.

Consider:

- Your readers – will they be sufficiently hooked by the name/celebrity status of your interviewees, and the knowledge they can impart, to buy the book?
- A series of books on a range of subjects, with different interviewees, appealing to different (or similar) markets.
- How a book of this kind is going to achieve what you want in terms of showcasing your niche expert status. To do it well, as Sue Stockdale has in her two books, you need to create some kind of synthesis of ideas to come up with a unique framework, set of principles or series of steps.
- How you can ensure your book serves your interviewees' interests too. As above, some may expect a cut of your royalties or a fee. Others will appreciate, at least, a biographical blurb with a link to their website to help promote their business.

Mapping out your book

'When you plan your book, you put the key question on a large sheet of paper and explore all of the connected questions people in your micro niche might ask.'
DANIEL PRIESTLEY, *BECOME A KEY PERSON OF INFLUENCE*

Joe's first business was website design and one of the first things he did with clients was to map out all the content using primary, secondary and tertiary levels. Of course, some sites go much deeper than this, but for a business or self-help book, where the same principle holds, stick to three levels maximum.

Everybody has different ways of planning, plotting and manipulating information. Most people work with one main, or two particularly strong elements of the VARK (visual, auditory, reading/writing, kinaesthetic) spectrum.

Lucy, as a writer and editor, majors in visual/reading/writing processing, so works in words, on paper or screen, in a linear format with headings and sub-headings to plan her books. Knowing that she won't get it right first time, she likes to leave lots of white space between lines and paragraphs, wide margins and room everywhere for more notes and crossings out.

Joe, as a graphic designer, is primarily visual. He enjoys mind-mapping and using physical elements to arrange the outline of his books. This is his favourite way to map out a book visually so it's easy to plot progress and plan his writing:

1. Get a massive sheet of paper or loads of squares of scrap paper and a big table, so you can re-order stuff easily.
2. Map out your main big picture themes and topics first. These will become your primary headings, chapters or sections. Leave the essential elements such as Foreword,

Acknowledgements, Praise, Introduction and About The Author, out of this map – we will discuss these later.

3. For each main topic add sub-topics. These will be your secondary headings or sub-chapters. Write these as if you're writing a headline for an article, which will come in handy when it comes to promoting your book anyway.

4. Optionally, for each sub-topic, map out any tertiary level topics. These are often just keywords to enable you to further split the subject down into manageable chunks for your audience.

You can see how the map for this book shaped up by viewing the Contents section – which shows two levels of headings. Try not to get into a fourth level of detail; if you do, it's a good indication your structure has become over-complex. Likewise, avoid 'nested lists' – lists or bullet points within lists/bullet points.

You will also see from the Contents page – and indeed that of any other book – that eventually every book structure has to be turned into a list. That is the nature of printed and, for the moment, e-books. So whether, like Joe, you like to mind-map first, or go straight to list, like Lucy, your book structure will end up as a linear plan, and it is best to get it into this format before you start writing. If you are submitting a proposal to a publisher, which could happen before you finish writing the book, it will need to include a detailed contents page. This form of document will also show you where you're strong on content, where you may need to carry out further research, and where you risk going into too much detail.

Make sure your plan allows for a certain amount of flexibility as you may well find you want to change the placement or order of some aspects when you start writing.

Your business or self-help book blueprint

> *'Take it from me – the more effort you put into planning and structuring, the easier it will be to write your book in the end.'*
> SUZAN ST MAUR, HOWTOWRITEBETTER.NET

The approach and outline we share on the following pages has worked well for many of our other authors. It should enable you to write your book in a paint-by-numbers way, meaning not that it will be rudimentary and basic, but that by sticking to a classic formula you can get on with the job of writing (and sharing what you know) and get it done quickly. This is just one way to do it, though, so feel free to tweak the blueprint for your own needs.

Introduction

It usually works best to write your Introduction at the end, after you know exactly what your book contains and how it will work for a reader. When you do write it, consider including content which covers these areas:

Why you should read this book

Make your big promise here, give anecdotes about other people who might be like your readers, including yourself. Prove the success you've had. Give figures and real examples where possible.

Who this book is for

If your book is aimed at one or more niche markets, you might want to quickly define the types of reader you will be talking to, what their main problem/question is and how you are going to solve/answer it in the book. Be careful not to exclude a wider market by defining your intended readership too closely.

My story

Let the reader know that you too were once where they are now. The story of your success will build credibility (so it's important that they know you're no longer 'that person'), but a story about how you first failed, had doubts, struggled and yet succeeded against the odds, using the method you're about to share with them, makes a much more compelling read. Write authentically and be genuine. Let other people say why you're great (that's why there should be a Praise section) and stick to the facts. Don't go into too much detail as your story should also be threaded through the entire book, not confined to the Introduction.

Chapter-by-chapter

Give a brief chapter-by-chapter commentary on what they'll be getting as a result of reading your business or self-help book. If you can't make a compelling promise/headline for any chapter then rethink the purpose/direction of that chapter until you can.

How to use this book

Not always necessary, but if they can choose whether to read from start to finish or pick relevant parts; or if you plan to provide exercises or actions at the end of each chapter, then tell them their options or your preferred approach.

The 3Ts

The 3Ts is known in fiction and drama as the three-act structure, but more simply involves ensuring that your book and every section, chapter and sub-section has a clearly defined Beginning-Middle-End structure. This particularly applies to each chapter of a business or self-help book – though should also be used to format shorter pieces from articles and blog posts to emails and letters.

T1. Tell them what you're going to tell them. Give the big picture and/or set the scene.

T2. Tell them. The main part of your book/chapter/article/post in which you present all the information, adding in the necessary detail and lead logically from one point to the next. T2 is the substantive part of your piece and may include sections with their own sub-headings.

T3. Tell them what you've told them – summarise and recap; if appropriate include a call to action. This could be a succinct paragraph, a bulleted list or a set of exercises – and where appropriate should lead the reader into the next chapter or section.

Chapter Structure

It's important to have a consistent and, where appropriate, identical structure for every single chapter in your book. Having the structure set in stone before you begin will really help keep things on target. Here's a suggested structure:

In this chapter

As in the 3Ts, **T1**: start each chapter by telling the reader what you are going to tell them. Either write a summary, introductory paragraph, or provide a bullet point list of the key topics/themes/things you'll cover.

3 – 6 Key Headings

T2: Tell the reader the key information. You will already have mapped out your sub-headings for each chapter – three areas are a minimum to cover; more than six becomes too much for a single chapter. As you'll see shortly, each section should be written like an individual article, with its own 3T structure – beginning, middle and end.

Optional extras

Depending on your subject and the business or self-help book archetype you are working to, each chapter might also include some or all of:

Case Studies/Examples – two to five per chapter. Keep them short and snappy, telling a story of people the reader can identify with (you or people you have worked with) and make sure they really illustrate the point you are making.

Exercises – restrict these to a few yes/no or self-scoring questions to focus the reader's mind on your point and its applicability to them. We wouldn't advise you to create the sort of exercises where you ask readers to fill in long answers on a blank page. They rarely stop to do this while they are reading. Asking them to do so can be off-putting, wastes space in your book and would not even work, of course, on Kindle or audio books

Breakout boxes – this is a technical term for pieces of text you might want to highlight or discriminate from the main narrative in some way. It might be a quotation, a reminder, a short list – anything that could add visual interest to a page. Two to four of these per chapter (perhaps one per subsection) is likely to be enough – less is usually more. Do not put these elements in actual boxes in your manuscript; just indicate the section, or the beginning and end. Any 'design' features you put into the manuscript will have to be removed by the editor or typesetter and replaced with their own design later.

Illustrations – graphs, charts, line drawings etc. should be in a hi-res format and designed to reproduce well in black and white. Consider whether you need these to help to illustrate your points, business models and ideas, or whether they're just decorative. We wouldn't advise you to include illustrations just for the sake of it and if you wish to inject humour with cartoons remember that what people find funny is subjective.

Summary

T3: tell the reader what you've just told them and what they should now know; set out what they should now be able to do or actions they should take as a result of this new knowledge. If this seems like a repeat of the opening to the chapter, it is, but it will be in the past tense rather than the future, which reinforces the key points and is proven to improve retention and recall of information.

Afterword or Summary

A simple chapter that reminds people of your key points, brings things together and leads them to take action and use what they've learned, is a good way to finish off a book and not leave your reader hanging. Remind people of all the vital information they've just learned with a positive summary (it will also help sell copies too, as prospective readers often go to the back to have a quick skim before buying). Tell them how they may think and feel now they've successfully completed your book. Simply telling people that they can feel pleased with themselves, happy, successful, relieved or proud will get that very response in many cases.

Once you've reminded them of all the high quality knowledge you've just shared, and told them they can feel great about how much better their life is now they've read your book, you can also tell them what to do next.

In marketing this is called your MWR (Most Wanted Response) so, while they're enjoying their high from finishing your book, you can lead them somewhere, perhaps to a sign-up form for other valuable free content on your website, or to contact you personally.

Four essential elements for a business or self-help book

All business or self-help books should contain the following sections in addition to the chapters containing the main content:

- Praise
- Foreword/Introduction
- Acknowledgements
- Author Biography

Praise

Also known as social proof, this is one of the most persuasive pieces of marketing content your prospective buyers will read. What other people say about you is always taken more seriously by your potential readers than what you say about yourself.

You'll be relying on other people to get back to you, though, so start soliciting praise as early as possible. While you can't expect people to write praise for a book that's not written yet, you can still get in touch with people you really admire or trust and ask them to agree to 'take a look' and write something for your book before it goes to print.

Good praise will say specific things about how your book solves a problem, makes people think differently or could change the reader's life in some tangible way.

If you're writing a book on something you've been doing for a long time (your business or a skill you have) then there's absolutely nothing wrong with including 'praise for the author' from your clients and people who've benefited from your advice over the years too.

Praise quotes to be featured at the start of your book should be no longer than a short paragraph, 'signed' by the writer and with their position, company and sometimes website underneath.

Praise quotes for the front or back cover of a book should be a single, or at most two, brief sentences, also signed (but without contact details).

Foreword

As we've described, a good Introduction is an essential part of any book. It is written by you, the author, and explains to the reader why you wrote the book, your credentials for writing it, and what they will gain from reading the book. It often works well to tell a good story – your story – here, and can be more personal than the rest of the book.

A Foreword is a different thing, and written by someone other than the author. If you have identified someone who you would like to write a Foreword, approach them early on when you can give them an outline of the book; they may write something for you ahead of reading the manuscript, but make sure you send them a finished – and, ideally, edited – manuscript before publication.

A good Foreword should:

- Be written by a known name, authority, expert or celebrity that your readers and prospective readers will either know, or admire and trust because of their position.
- Focus on the benefits of your book to the reader from the perspective of the authority writing it.
- Make reference to why the Foreword writer is qualified to comment on, and recommend the advice in, your book.

Acknowledgements

This is essential to acknowledge the people who've helped you on your journey to publication. With their names in print in your book, these people will also feel more committed to helping you market and promote your book.

Thank people who have generally helped: your publisher (especially if you're hoping to publish more books with them), specific members of the publishing team; the person who wrote your Foreword; and Test readers (beta readers) who have read and given feedback on your manuscript; colleagues, mentors, clients, friends, people who gave you praise etc. Family may come into this list too, but if you're using this tactically, mention your partner, kids, parents etc. in a dedication instead.

Thank people who have inspired you: this can include other authors and big names. Include a website link where possible so they gain a tangible benefit from the mention. Their name in your book may make them more inclined to help you if you find yourself in a position to ask them for an endorsement or mention to their contacts.

Acknowledgements used to be placed at the front of a book, but with the advent of the online Look Inside feature, publishers realised that they take up valuable front pages through which potential readers check out the book content, so now they are mostly found at the back of books.

Author Biography

This is the place to really lay out your credentials, professional history and qualifications. Ask yourself, 'Why am I uniquely qualified to write this book and why should readers listen to what I have to say?'

Some people write a whole résumé here, but it's much better if you can summarise the relevant parts of your story including where you either overcame an obstacle or stumbled upon the secrets you're sharing in the book.

Also feature aspects like how long you've been an expert on your subject, what your success consists of, how many TV, radio and magazine appearances you've got and anything else that lets readers know you're an authority.

This is the place to invite readers to make contact with you through your website (also mention free offers to readers here), social media or however else you are open to communication. Be careful of including your email address.

Back Cover Essentials

Your final piece of writing to complete your business or self-help book is the back cover. The wording on it – the sales blurb – needs to work hard to sell the book. To achieve this you need four elements, which should be short and sweet.

1. **The Sales Blurb.** This should say who the book is for (could be phrased as 'For people who want...'), what they'll get (your big promise) and why they should buy it and read it now. Keep this brief and condensed.
2. **Bullets of Benefits.** Whether you use these words or not, this list should answer the question, 'What will you learn from reading this book?' This is your chance to make your big promises and paraphrase the best bits from your table of contents to whet the reader's appetite in four or five bullet points.
3. **Praise.** Some back covers have nothing but praise; however, this can look like overkill and a couple, or even just one piece of key praise from a well known expert, backed up with a little sales blurb, works best. One or two

very short sentences is as much as is needed for back cover praise quotes.

4. **Author Bio.** Just three or four sentences focused on why you are uniquely qualified to write this book. Your full bio is on the inside back page; on the back cover just list your most relevant credentials, qualifications and key element of your story, but don't waste space on unrelated details. Always remember the reader is looking for what's in it for them to read your book. Include a photograph (professional headshot) if there's room because it personalises the book and can help to raise the author's profile.

Summary

Having worked through this section, you will now know which book archetype will best suit your content and communication style. You understand the value of creating a blueprint for your book by first unpacking the content through mind-mapping, then developing a detailed, linear structure in the form of your Contents Page.

You will be able to incorporate the 3Ts in every piece of writing within your book, and structure each chapter so the reader can best absorb its content. You know what additional elements will provide light and shade in your book, such as case studies and breakout boxes. You're aware of the extras that top and tail a professional book.

With all the planning done and dusted, it's time to actually get writing your business or self-help book.

Writing
Your Book

3

WRITING YOUR BOOK

Now you've completed the planning stages, we're going to work through the process of writing step-by-step and in detail.

This is where many first time authors lose their way. They may know who their market is, have crafted a brilliant title and worked out what they want to say in what order – but the tasks of writing, checking, re-writing, editing… become overwhelming and they give up. The main reason for this is that new writers think they have to write a perfect book at first draft; this is absolutely not what you should be aiming for.

Writing a book is made up of a series of discrete tasks which, if carried out one by one and in the right order, makes it simple (if not easy!) to create a great business or self-help book.

We developed the A.U.T.H.O.R. model to help our authors plan and structure their book, and use our W.R.I.T.E.R. process to take them through a logical and organised writing process.

Here are the steps we work through:

We will outline each of them in turn. Additionally, in this section we will be helping you to:

- Choose a voice and tone for your book – friendly, business-like, encouraging, etc – so you can stay in character throughout.
- Use the W.R.I.T.E.R. Process to create your book through a discrete series of actions, rather than getting bogged down trying to do everything in one go.
- Decide on and stick to a consistent set of rules for structuring, writing and formatting.
- Understand the basic grammar of sentence construction and punctuation – don't worry, we'll make it simple for you.

'Never give up. And most importantly, be true to yourself. Write from your heart, in your own voice, and about what you believe in.'

LOUISE BROWN

Your writing style

The style of writing can make a big difference to the position of your book and the impact it has on you and your business, as well as on your readers. Our joint style is (we hope) informal, friendly, and generally positive and encouraging. Inevitably this will work for some people and possibly annoy others, but it's genuinely us, and therefore most likely to come across as authentic.

If you're planning to be seen as a serious authority, it may be best to take a more sober, balanced and less chatty approach, but the cost could be a book that is harder to read (for some people) and a slower pace. Some authors seem more comfortable telling detailed stories that eventually get to a point, while others tell you the punch line first and then fill in the detail. While you should write in a style that puts across your personality, if you have conversational tics (like rambling, getting side-tracked or repeating the same phrases), look out for these in your writing style where you have more chance of correcting them before they start to bore your readers.

Your core voice

In order to guard against over-formal or pretentious writing, new writers are often advised to 'write how you speak'. While this idea helps ensure that your text is natural and congruent with the 'real you', if you pasted into your book a slab of your real-life speech, it would seem unfocused, long-winded, boring and would appear – strangely –

unnatural. If you've ever tried to read verbatim transcripts of interviews, you'll know how hard they are to plough through. Readers don't want to see in print the ums and ers, pauses, digressions and waffling that everyday chat consists of.

We also all have very lazy habits in speech that make for difficult reading when you transfer them to the page. Most of us don't construct our spoken sentences efficiently to get information across in the clearest way. We can rely on our facial expression, body language and context to add meaning to our words whilst talking directly to someone, but when you're engaging through written material it's 100% words.

There's definitely a benefit in getting into a particular mindset or persona when you write (which may not be the same as your usual private self) in order to make your book stronger. Here are few voice characteristics you might want to adopt or avoid:

Opinionated, Ranting, Cheeky, Jocular, Serious, Authoritative, Inclusive, Instructive, Supportive, Aggressive, Tough, Soft, Friendly, Energetic, Calm, Considered, Balanced, Nice, Self-Deprecating, Persuasive, Excited, Humorous, Encouraging, Optimistic, Pessimistic, Sceptical…

Write as yourself

If you're a first time author, you may feel tempted to adopt a writing style that you think gives you more gravitas than the way you would normally communicate. You really don't need to do this; in fact you definitely should not do this, as readers want to feel personally involved with the authentic you, and not be lectured by some academic or business guru.

'You and your purpose in life are the same thing.
Your purpose is to be you.'
GEORGE ALEXIOU

Writing that tries to be too clever comes across as self-conscious and the reader will often feel embarrassed by the author's fumbling attempts to impress. Most people read a book firstly because they want the information it contains or, more specifically, the benefits it promises; and secondly because they believe and trust that the author is someone who can give them that. If what you're writing is genuine, unambiguous and easy to read, you've given the reader what they want.

While you don't want to make spelling, punctuation and grammatical errors that will cause irritated readers to post sarcastic reviews on your Amazon page, you shouldn't worry too much about getting it all right – especially in your first draft. There's a quick and easy section on grammar and punctuation coming up, but in the first instance concentrate on your message more than the medium. And remember, no book should ever be published without a professional copy-editor having worked rigorously through it to weed out any errors the author might have left in.

Clear and simple

'...Use plain, simple language, short words and brief sentences. That is the way to write English – it is the modern way and the best way. Stick to it; don't let fluff and flowers and verbosity creep in.'

MARK TWAIN

Lucy was once given the best advice by an editor, who told her, 'Be kind to your readers'. It's in your interest for readers to enjoy reading your book and not to feel as though it's hard work to understand or an uphill battle to get through. If there's a hard way or an easy way to say something, use the easy way. If there's a long way or a short way to describe something, take the short route. Avoid technical jargon unless you really don't have a choice. Do your reader a favour by keeping it crystal clear and by not assuming they have your level of knowledge – they are reading your book precisely because they do not, so make sure your points are easy to understand. If you need to use an obscure word or an acronym, provide a definition or spell it out in full the first time you use it. If you have to use, and they need to learn, specialist terms, consider including a glossary at the back of the book so they can always look up what they aren't familiar with.

Check out some of the top business or self-help books in any field. Most of them use simple language and construction to tell their stories – which, when done well, is the height of sophistication.

Closely related to the use of simple language is clarity of approach. Never say something in three steps if it can be said just as easily in one. This is just creating filler and, while it makes your book bigger, can make your readers give up on you.

If you have a really important and perhaps complex point to make, explain it in one or two different ways, which could include a simple tool, series of bullet points or a graphic image. Some people understand best through words alone, others like to visualise, and yet others need a very concrete explanation to make sense of concepts.

Finally, don't mix your metaphors. If you're talking about 'ballpark figures' then don't also mention 'the writing on the wall' and that somebody's 'boat has just come in'. See what we have to say about clichés shortly and you'll avoid most of these traps anyway.

Know your audience

Is your content for beginners or experts? Is your audience likely to be made up of lay people or industry professionals?

Covering all the basics in a book for boffins will bore them into oblivion so consider including the basics in a reference section, refer them to simpler books or make it clear this stuff is here as a refresher. Likewise, assuming that a lay reader knows the background and talking about high level concepts without covering the basics first will alienate the reader.

Make it clear who your book is for and what level of skill or knowledge you're assuming they have from the outset, on the cover if possible, and your job of writing the book will be made easier. It will free you from having to dumb down your advanced information and you can focus on creating a book your readers will love. It will also allow you to skip the more complicated stuff while ensuring your readers feel they're getting what you promised.

If in doubt, cover the essential basics first and excuse yourself by explaining that many readers will know this already so they can skip it.

Metaphorical or literal

Sometimes a well-chosen metaphor can say something far more elegantly than page after page of literal description. It's often more quotable, more interesting and more efficient than being literal. The easiest way to come up with metaphors is to think of an existing pattern, observation or problem and ask yourself, 'What else is that like?'

Here's a much quoted one that's been attributed to Virginia Woolf, among others, and makes the point:

> *'Writing is like sex. First you do it for love, then you do it for your friends, and then you do it for money.'*

Good metaphors are emotive because the comparison is so much more dramatic than any amount of literal reasoning could be. Over-use of metaphors, or tenuous, or mixed metaphors, though, can distort the facts by over-generalising and over-simplifying an issue. You could use one as an overall framework for the book: e.g. 'A Recipe For A Happier Life', then on a chapter-by-chapter basis, 'The Ingredients', 'The Right Equipment', 'Weighing and Measuring', 'Getting the Mix Right', 'Cooking with Gas'...; or sparingly, as an occasional attention-grabbing device, and back them up with more detailed and literal argument.

Avoid clichés like the plague

> *'Be a first rate version of yourself, not a second rate version of someone else.'*
> JUDY GARLAND

Clichés are often difficult to avoid because they have become so much a part of the normal, idiomatic way we speak that we hardly notice them. However, clichés in writing are dangerous because either readers ignore them, or they've become so commonplace they've lost any power to engage your reader. Either way, they make your writing sound lazy and unoriginal. Business, social media, marketing and psychological jargon very quickly becomes clichéd, so check your writing for these kinds of cliché and find other – probably simpler, but more accurate – ways to make your point.

Playing with or subverting existing clichés is fine if you can come up with something that makes the reader stop, maybe smile and take notice of what you're saying.

Make it your job when you review your work to look for clichéd words and phrases, and either repurpose them or simply remove them completely. Your own original words and descriptions are more quotable and mark out your writing and thinking as fresh and memorable.

How long should a business or self-help book be?

The length – or word count – of your book is important for a number of reasons. First, business or self-help books win over fiction and narrative nonfiction because they can be shorter and yet perceived as (and therefore priced at) higher value. An average novel is 80,000 words, but in paperback is likely to be priced at under £10. The average business or self-help book is under 40,000 words, but likely to be priced at £12 or more.

In our experience, readers of business or self-help titles want a solution to their problem or answer to their question quickly and practically. They want to soak up the information from the book like a sponge, then be able to go off and put it into action. They don't want a book that is going to take them several weeks to read (unlike a summer read novel or analytical history book) and are likely to give up reading it if you present them with one, which means they will never understand your full message or be able to make effective use of it.

We would advise you to think in terms of 30,000 to 40,000 words. Some self-help books, which could be structured around a daily homily, or a monthly activity can be dense but brief, between 20,000 and 30,000 words. Less than 20,000 words, though, makes for a very slim book or a very large typeface.

Others, such as technical tutorials, might be action and info-packed and run up to 60,000 words, as the reader might only need to pick the elements they need and not read the entire text.

40,000 words is a safe and workable average that offers enough solid content without making the reader work too hard or too long.

THE W.R.I.T.E.R. PROCESS

1. **Write** – Working from your Book Plan, get your words out onto the page. Fill out everything in your structure with all the content you can bring to it. The first draft doesn't have to be brilliantly written, it just has to be written. Limit your self-editing and internal critic in order to produce the quantity of content you require.

"Don't get it right – get it written!"
LEE CHILD

2. **Review** – Don't mistake this step for proof-reading; reviewing is looking through your book with the perspective of a reader rather than a writer. Print out your first draft and read through the paper copy; this will give you distance and a more objective reading

experience. Look for any gaps, repetitions, inconsistencies or obvious errors and make notes. Check the word count and note where content needs to be removed. Any material you trim from your main book may still come in handy later for an article, blog post, press release or content for another chapter, so don't feel it's going to waste.

3. **Improve** – Go back to your electronic manuscript and work through your book a chapter at a time, using your hard copy Review notes, to add, remove, re-order or sharpen up content. You can work on your style, too, but this is not your main focus at the moment. When you've done as much as you can on one chapter, stop and move onto the next. Again, it doesn't have to be perfect.

4. **Test** – It's time to get some feedback on your improved first draft. Ask no more than six trusted colleagues, clients, authors or anyone who falls within the potential market of your book, to read and give you honest feedback – both positive and developmental. If possible, give them a deadline to get back to you and an idea of some key responses you would like from each individual. Take all feedback as a useful learning experience – the criticism is often more useful than the praise.

5. **Edit** – Process all the suggestions made by your 'beta readers' and decide which to implement. Make structural or major content changes first. Then print your manuscript out and proof read it in hard copy; you will pick up more errors this way.

> Finally, work through your document slowly, checking each sentence, as well as paragraph, section and chapter, for sense and structure, and implement all your hard copy proofing.
>
> 6. **Repeat** Steps 4 and 5 as often as necessary. Editing should take at least as long as the initial writing process. Seriously consider paying for a professional edit before submitting your manuscript even to a traditional publisher. A professional edit is essential if you are self-publishing. A reputable traditional or hybrid publisher will include a copy-edit as part of the publishing process.

Write your book like a series of articles

Check this book's contents page and you'll see a pattern. It reads like a series of articles on all kinds of subjects that authors and would-be authors will be interested in. This is not an accident; it's a deliberate design feature, because…

We now have a whole archive of content we can cherry-pick and repurpose as articles, blog posts, courses, videos and press releases, to promote *How To Write Your Book Without The Fuss* and attract other business.

The Contents page (something almost everyone checks out before buying a book) becomes a powerful selling tool in its own right.

The Contents page and all the headings in the book are packed with relevant keywords that help it get picked up in search engines (like *http://books.google.com*) and online bookstores (like *www.amazon.com*).

Each chapter was easy to write with a clear focus because we wrote the book one article at a time.

Write your book chapter by chapter

Once you've mapped out the blueprint of your entire book, it's a good idea to treat each chapter as a unique project in its own right. With your detailed chapter outline you can set yourself a series of achievable goals and timeframes on the way to getting your whole book written, rather than one dauntingly large one. If you are writing to a deadline (self-imposed or external), the time you spend on the first chapter will give you a clear idea of how long the rest of the book is likely to take – though the good news is that once you get into the writing habit, your skill and speed will improve.

Although it applies to the writing of your entire book, the first three steps of the W.R.I.T.E.R. process – Write, Review, Improve – can be used on every individual chapter if you prefer to work that way. Take these activities one at a time: complete the first draft of each chapter before you Review; Review to the end before you go back to Improve.

It's usually best to write the chapters in the order they come in, to get the logical progression right, but if you get bogged down in one chapter, leave it and move on to the next. It will either become clear what needs to go before, or it may demonstrate a need to rework some of your outline.

The chapter-writing process

List all the headings and sub-headings for the chapter (refer back to your book blueprint. See 'Mapping out your book').

You should already have decided in your blueprint on a total word count for the book as a whole, and for each chapter. Now allocate the total chapter word count between the sub-headings, leaving some over for the intro and summary (the 3Ts). Sub-sections don't have to be exactly the same length, but it will help you avoid over-writing if you have a target in mind, and readers find it easier to work through your book if you set up consistent structural expectations for them.

Go back to the start of your chapter and write a chapter introduction: it should spell out what people are going to learn and set the scene. Decide, in your first one, on a consistent style for chapter intros – will you tell readers what the chapter will teach them in a narrative form; in a bullet-pointed list; as a quotation, at some length or very briefly… ?

Treat each sub-heading as a unique, stand-alone article and write the content for each one using the **T3** Format.

T1. Tell them what you're going to tell them. Give the big picture and/or set the scene.

T2. Tell them. Add in all the necessary detail and, where possible, point towards the next subject for extra polish.

T3. Tell them what you've told them – summarise and recap; if appropriate include a call to action.

If you need to clarify a point with a chart, table or illustration, make a note of what you want – but don't stop to find or create it, keep on writing. Include case studies, examples, breakout boxes and quotes if you have them to hand; if not, leave a note for yourself to fill them in later – don't break the writing flow to do research or check your records. Keep writing.

Once you've finished writing each chapter you can choose to either Review and Improve before moving onto the next chapter, or keep going and Review and Improve your whole book in one fell sweep at the end of your first draft.

Know your daily and early word count targets

'When asked, "How do you write?" I invariably answer, "One word at a time," and the answer is invariably dismissed. But that is all it is.'

STEVEN KING

A 40,000 word manuscript can seem daunting if it's not tackled correctly so it's important to break it down into manageable chunks and to ensure your deadline is realistic. Here's how:

1. Map out your book so that you know how many chapters it will contain and all the chunks of information you require.
2. Know your target word count for the whole book.
3. Know your deadline.
4. Work backwards from your deadline and count how many days you have available (don't forget to allow for

breaks). This should give you a rough daily or weekly word count target.

5. Now divide this figure by the number of productive hours you are able, in terms of time and focus, to write in a day to get your hourly word count target. We suggest that an average of 1,000 words per hour is reasonable when working through a first draft (without revising or improving) from your detailed book structure

6. Is your target realistic, achievable or possible? If not you may need to re-adjust your deadline or, if the deadline is immovable, you're going to have to put in longer days until the hourly word count figure is manageable.

'I found the hardest part about writing the book was the discipline of keeping to deadlines and making the time to write in two-hour sessions. I had a strict diarised schedule of 5am starts to make sure I could write and not impact on my working day. Writing a book needs careful and thorough planning and the discipline to set and achieve deadlines. It sounds daunting, but it is possible and I have read some great books by new authors in the past year that have been really helpful in my business. Writing is worth the effort – giving someone one piece of advice that they take from your book and use to make their company or life better is a really good feeling.'

LOUISE WALKER, AUTHOR *FROM THE GROUND UP*

Grammar Lesson

We apologise if this seems like a trip back to school days, but in our experience many writers, especially those whose expertise is in their own subject rather than writing itself, have forgotten some basic rules of grammar and punctuation. It makes writing and reading a book much easier if the author is fluent in the basic rules of constructing sentences and paragraphs, and punctuating them correctly. The way these are taught in school is not always entirely correct, or easy to apply, so bear with us and work your way through some ideas that might make your writing life easier.

Structuring a sentence

Your writing should communicate your meaning to the reader with maximum ease and clarity. Although we've talked about finding your authentic and individual writing voice, you will appeal to the widest readership if you align this with 'Standard English'.

To do this, it's essential to use punctuation correctly and form sentences that comply with basic rules of grammar. Grammar and punctuation are tools of good communication. They provide a window through which the reader 'sees' your point of view: well-written narrative gives the reader such a clear view that they are not even aware of the glass through which they are looking; mis-punctuated writing with poor grammatical construction is like a dirty window, by which the reader is constantly distracted, and through which they peer with difficulty in order to 'see' what's going on.

"A sentence should be read as if its author, had he held a plough instead of a pen, could have drawn a furrow deep and straight to the end."

HENRY DAVID THOREAU

Let's go back to basics.

The sentence is the fundamental building block of written communication. A sentence can be short or long, but its essential components are:

- to start with a capital letter
- to end with a *full stop/period*, and
- to contain a *subject and verb* (the subject is a noun or pronoun who/that carries out the verb)

'I do.' or 'I am.' are perhaps the shortest possible, if not the most elegant, sentences in the English language.

An author is considered an expert.
Writing a book is hard work.
A published book attracts income. (This last has an object, *income,* as well as a subject.)

These are all complete, grammatical **simple sentences**. They comprise a single, independent clause.

Imperative sentences, such as exclamations (*Hello!*), commands (*Get moving!*), and requests (*Please sit down.*), are the only exceptions to the subject/verb sentence rule – though they imply both: *I bid you hello; Would you get moving; Will you please sit down.*

Simple sentences, like all those above, generally need no further punctuation. A simple sentence is ideal for punchy statements and giving a direct, instructional feel to your message, but your readers would quickly tire of an entire book written like this. With more complex sentence structures comes the greater need to punctuate carefully for sense and readability.

Compound Sentences are easy enough: they are essentially two related, simple sentences stuck together with a conjunction, such as 'and', 'but', 'or', 'because', 'although', etc..

An author is considered an expert and books attract income.

This compound sentence, composed of two independent clauses (which could each be a stand-alone sentence), doesn't require any internal punctuation. If, though, you add a third clause –

An author is considered an expert and books attract income, but writing a book is hard work.

– adding a comma after the second clause makes it easier for the reader to comprehend.

As a general rule (though there are exceptions, one of which is the Oxford comma), do *not* put a comma before an 'and'; always put a comma before 'but'.

To join two related clauses/sentences *without* a conjunction – and so create a more enigmatic sentence – use a **semi-colon**.

An author is considered an expert and books attract income; writing a book is hard work.

It is incorrect to use a semi-colon with a conjunction, so you would *not* write: *An author is considered an expert and books attract income; but writing a book is hard work.*

Compound sentences are useful for connecting facts, but you need more variation than simple and compound sentences to express more involved ideas and situations.

Complex Sentences can, if clearly structured, be the most dynamic and information-packed kind of sentence. The simplest complex sentence consists of a main clause and a dependent clause. The main clause can stand alone, but dependent clauses, as their name suggests, don't work without a main clause.

An author is considered an expert, because writing a book is hard work, and books attract income.

Here, *An author is considered an expert* is the main clause, while *because writing a book is hard work* is the sub-clause (and doesn't stand alone).

The key to punctuating complex sentences is knowing where to place the commas. This is *not*, as you may have been used to believing, about inserting a comma where you would pause when speaking. It *is* about separating the sub-clause(s) from the main clause. The sub-clause can come at the start or end of a complex sentence; in either case it only needs one comma to separate it off:

Because we know that writing a book is hard work, an author is considered an expert.

An author is considered an expert, *because we know that writing a book is hard work.*

If you place the sub-clause in the middle of the sentence, though, it must be separated by a comma on both sides:

An author, *because we know that writing a book is hard work,* is considered an expert.

Too often, writers omit one or both of the commas around a central sub-clause, making a sentence hard, if not nonsensical, to read:

An author because we know that writing a book is hard work is considered an expert.

Commas should be used in the same way to separate conjunctions: *However,* books attract income. Books attract income, *however.* Books, *however,* attract income.

At the peak of sentence complexity sits the **Complex-compound sentence**. As you may have guessed, this is a combination of compound and complex sentences. They have two or more main clauses, at least one dependent clause, and often need careful use of the full range of punctuation marks to make sense.

You can get the most information across and develop more detailed ideas using complex or complex-compound sentences, but simple and compound sentences are good for straightforward facts, and conveying information clearly. For business or self-help, we suggest conservative use of complex-compound sentences because they increase the likelihood that readers will misinterpret (or be forced to re-read) your message. Sentences in business or self-help writing should be kept to around 20 words or less, in the interests of clarity and ease of reading.

Building A Paragraph

Having talked about different kinds of sentence structure, and how to punctuate a sentence, let's now look at combining sentences to form paragraphs – and a little more punctuation.

If sentences are the building blocks of written communication, paragraphs are the panels, doors and windows in the walls of your informational edifice.

So, what is a paragraph?

A paragraph is a group of one or more sentences. By starting on a new line, each paragraph is separated from the last one. A paragraph concludes with the appropriate punctuation mark at the end of its final sentence, which often falls in the middle of a line of text. Like a sentence, therefore, a paragraph can end with a full stop/period, question or exclamation mark, closed inverted commas, a dash or ellipsis (three – exactly – dots, followed by a space...) or carriage return before the first word of the next sentence (or paragraph).

(It could also finish with a closing bracket, but bracketed sentences shouldn't appear too often in a business or self-help book.)

In a printed book, paragraphs can be indented on the first line (except at the start of a chapter or section), have 'trailing spaces' after the end of the last sentence (i.e., the last line is not justified to the right), but are not separated from the paragraph above or below by a line space.

When formatting paragraphs in your manuscript, however, bear in mind that, for technical reasons, most editors and publishers prefer authors *not* to indent the first line of a paragraph (though if you do indent, use the tab key and not the space bar); a line space between paragraphs is also preferred.

What are paragraphs for?

Paragraphs have a physical purpose: they act as a visual break for readers, separating the text into distinct and variable-sized blocks, which help a reader keep their place on the page and also within the development of your structure. Pages of solid text, or very long paragraphs, are intimidating, tiring to read and don't draw the eye forwards through the information; too many short paragraphs, though, can make for a jerky and disrupted reading experience.

Just as sentences of differing lengths create changing rhythms for your content, so do varying-sized paragraphs. Longer paragraphs usually indicate detailed description or complex concepts, so the delivery becomes slower and more measured as readers work their way through them.

Shorter paragraphs happen around quick, attention-grabbing thoughts, rapid action and the introduction of vital information. An occasional paragraph of a single sentence, or even one word can have a more immediate and powerful effect than several longer paragraphs. Shorter paragraphs can be used to shock the reader or to make a sharp or sudden point, but should be used sparingly so as not to dissipate their potency.

A good mix of paragraphs of differing lengths keeps the reader engaged and varies the speed and tone of your writing. Look at this page and see where your eye is attracted to short, punchy paragraphs in the first instance and how, while you are reading longer ones, you are drawn into more complex ideas and concepts.

When should you start a new paragraph?

1. **When one piece of information, explanation or thought finishes**, the new subject matter should start with a new paragraph. If you are covering a protracted concept or idea, use an introductory paragraph; an ending, or summary, paragraph; and as many paragraphs as you need to delineate the stages between.

2. **When the focus of your explanation changes** – especially if you are changing from one point of view to another (e.g. the author's to the reader's) – begin a new paragraph.

3. **When none of the above apply and you are in the middle of a long section**, but you need to give your reader some incentives to get through it. In the same way as you punctuate a sentence to make it easy for your

reader to understand, break up your information into logical paragraphs, manageable bites or even bullet points, to give structure to your message, and visual variation on the page.

How do you structure a paragraph?

If you think of a paragraph as a frame for a certain amount of information, how to give it the right shape and form becomes clearer. Each paragraph is acting as a boundary for the related items within it. It can open with an introductory sentence, followed by others that expand on the opening point, and close with a sentence which sums up or completes the point (3Ts again). Just as a picture frame should be the best size and shape to display the painting it contains, so a paragraph should neatly contain the chunk of information being conveyed to the reader.

Read the previous paragraph again and note how it is shaped in this way.

How to order paragraphs

Dividing your text into well-formed paragraphs gives you a great opportunity to try out different ways of organising sections and chapters. We said at the start that paragraphs represent the panels, doors and windows of your text: just as an architect will design a beautiful and functional house by moving these elements around until they look and work best, so a writer can order and re-order paragraphs until they provide the clearest possible message.

An important thing to consider, when deciding which paragraph should go where, is the logic of the structure. What information does the reader need first and which aspects should be held back to make your case with the most impact? In most cases it is best to give the information in sequence. Place related paragraphs together and check whether they progress logically. Try changing the order and see whether this enhances the effect you are looking for.

It can take time to become really adept at using paragraphs to make your writing connect, so practise forming strong and logical paragraphs, which link to each other and/or break up sections, with everything you write. Paragraphs are a vital tool for the writer and act as signposts for the reader. Learn to use them to relay information, develop a convincing argument, reveal concepts and introduce important themes.

More Punctuation

In Lucy's experience as an editor, too many writers seem to think that the rules of grammar, particularly those of punctuation, get in the way of their ability to communicate authentically. However, the opposite is true: punctuation is there to enable you to convey your ideas clearly to your reader. Mis-punctuation can not only make your writing hard to understand, it can completely change the sense of what you want to say.

Here are a couple of examples – not original, but they make the point:

Let's eat Grandpa.

No, let's not; let's add a comma in the right place:

Let's eat, Grandpa.

Here's something a little more complex (in structure as well as meaning):

A woman without her man is nothing

If you punctuate this sentence with a couple of commas to create a subclause in the middle, it means one thing:

A woman, without her man, is nothing.

However, if you use a colon for expansion and add a comma to separate an opening clause, without altering a single word it means almost exactly the opposite:

A woman: without her, man is nothing.

The best way to remember the right applications of the different punctuations marks – and there aren't that many of them, after all – is to limit the situations in which you should use them. If you've stuck a comma in a sentence but it doesn't seem to be for one of these three main uses, it probably shouldn't be there.

Three Main Uses of Commas

1. Commas contain clauses

If in doubt about where to place commas in a sentence, remember the above subtitle. Commas should *not* be used, as is often taught in school, simply to indicate where a pause occurs in spoken speech. Understanding where to place a comma correctly is, more often than not, about separating the subclause from the main clause of a sentence.

When the subclause (in italics below) is placed at the start or end of a sentence, it only needs one comma to separate it from the main clause:

Despite having been neglected,
the garden was a riot of blossom.

The garden was a riot of blossom,
despite having been neglected.

But when the sub-clause falls in the middle of a sentence, it needs a comma either side to enclose it:

The garden, *despite having been neglected,*
was a riot of blossom.

In the sentence above it would probably be better to use no commas at all than to put only one before, or one after, the subclause.

2. **Commas separate qualifying words and phrases in a sentence** in exactly the same way:

> *However,* I'm delighted to say that…
> I'm delighted, *however,* to say that…

> *From my perspective,* it looks like… It looks, *from my perspective,* like… It looks like… , *from my perspective.*

3. **Commas separate items in a simple list,** e.g.:

When writing business or self-help it is important to be clear about your *chapters, sections, case studies, quotations* and *writing style.*

As a general rule, don't put a comma before 'and'; always put a comma before 'but'.

Link and Separate – the only two uses for the semi-colon

Too many writers avoid using semi-colons, a most delicate and subtle punctuation mark, because they don't know what they are for or where to place them. Equally, too many writers use semi-colons, wrongly believing they know where to use them, and cause a lot of work for editors. As there are only two main uses for a semi-colon, it's not too hard to remember.

1. **Semi-colons link two related clauses** which could otherwise be joined by a conjunction or separated by a period/full stop.

So, you might write: 'I love Paris. It is a beautiful city.' Or: 'I love Paris because it is a beautiful city.'

But more subtle and interesting is: *I love Paris; it is a beautiful city.*

Don't use a semi-colon to link two *unrelated* clauses – 'I love Paris; let's have pizza tonight.' would not be correct. *Don't* use a semi-colon *and* a conjunction to link two clauses – 'I love Paris; because it's a beautiful city.' is also incorrect.

2. **Semi-colons separate items on a complex list** (a list with long items and items that have internal punctuation, such as a comma).

The meeting consisted of *the Chair's introduction; a report from the Finance Director; a discussion about the budget, which became quite heated; and a vote on which way to proceed.*

In complex lists like this you would put a semi-colon before the final 'and', unlike at the end of a simple list separated by commas.

The Three Main Uses for Colons

Most people are pretty secure in their use of colons, though we have seen them used in place of a semi-colon, so let us remind you of:

1. **Definition or expansion** of an initial statement

I felt a sudden twinge: the wound in my knee was playing up.

In this case, the phrase following the colon should start

with a lower case word, unless it's 'I' or a proper name; or if the definition/expansion continues for more than one sentence.

1. To set up a quotation

Polonius tells Laertes: '... to thine own self be true.'

If the quote is more than one sentence long, it should start on a new line following the colon, and form an indented paragraph not enclosed in quotation marks.

2. To introduce a list

This recipe requires the following ingredients: 3 eggs, 6 oz flour, 6 oz sugar and 6 oz butter.

Items can also be numbered or bulleted following a colon. If the introductory phrase does not stand alone as a sentence, a colon is not required. *This recipe requires 3 eggs, 6 oz flour...*

The Two Main Uses of the Apostrophe

If you really want to irritate a reader or an editor, putting your apostrophes in the wrong place is a quick and easy way to do it. The first of these is obvious, but *do not* mess up your 'its' and your 'it's'. And take serious note of how to use a possessive apostrophe to meant what you intend it to.

"To those who care about punctuation, a sentence such as "Thank God its Friday" (without the apostrophe) rouses feelings not only of despair but of violence. The

confusion of the possessive "its" (no apostrophe) with the contractive "it's" (with apostrophe) is an unequivocal signal of illiteracy and sets off a Pavlovian "kill" response in the average stickler."

LYNNE TRUSS, *EATS, SHOOTS & LEAVES:*

THE ZERO TOLERANCE APPROACH TO PUNCTUATION

1. **To show where a word has been contracted and** a letter(s) left out

   Don't for 'do not'; *she'll* for 'she will'; *he's* for 'he is' or 'he has'.

   Simple enough, apart from using an apostrophe with the word 'it'. The possessive, *its,* has no apostrophe; **only put an apostrophe in** *it's* **when it's a contraction of 'it is'.**

2. **To denote possession – apostrophe+s**

   Anna's book (the book owned by Anna); *In a week's time* (within the period of a week).

   If the word ends in 's', whether it is plural (books) or is singular but ends in 's' (James), add the **apostrophe alone:** *The books' covers* (covers of the books); *James' coat* (the coat belonging to James). Plurals that do not end in 's' (e.g., women, children), take apostrophe+s in the possessive: *the women's bags, the children's toys.*

   Don't use an apostrophe to make a plural, even of acronyms or dates. The plural of PC is *PCs,* not PC's;

the flower power decade is *the 1960s,* not the 1960's. The Smith family are *the Smiths,* not *the Smith's.*

The end of the sentence

Finally, let's look at those alternative sentence endings, question and exclamation marks. It may seem obvious, but again it's surprising how often question marks are misplaced and added at the end of statements that are not questions. As for exclamation marks – delete, delete, delete. A full-length book rarely needs more than half a dozen exclamation marks in the whole manuscript; many more tells an editor or publisher that this is an amateur writer. As with adjectives and adverbs, less is more. Your choice of words and writing style should make it clear to a reader where your emphases fall or you are being humorous.

Question marks should only be used after direct questions:

How many copies will my book sell?

'I wonder how many copies my book will sell.' is a statement, not a question and should not have a question mark.

When it comes to exclamation marks, F. Scott Fitzgerald says it all:

'Cut out all those exclamation points. An exclamation point is like laughing at your own joke.'

If you really think one is necessary, make it one – never two or more. And if you must use both a question mark and exclamation mark together, it should be that way round: ?!

Immunising yourself against writers' block

Blocks can happen for all kinds of reasons. However, there are plenty of things you can do from the outset of your writing project *and* as you progress to minimise the risk and block-proof yourself.

Do things in the correct order. If you recall what we said earlier about on creativity then you'll know that it's difficult (if not impossible) to try to create ideas at the same time as editing them – it's the equivalent of speaking while attempting to listen. Well the same applies to writing too. So remember to do the right things at the right time… Using first the A.U.T.H.O.R. model, then the W.R.I.T.E.R. process, Plan/Map Out, Write, Review, Improve, Test and Edit as distinct and separate steps.

Create a vacuum that needs to be filled. The process of mapping out your book and then including all the empty headings for each chapter is a deliberate way to create a vacuum that you'll feel compelled to fill with new content. So don't skip the important planning steps or you could end up getting bogged down.

Clear your calculator. This is based on Maxwell Maltz's advice in his classic book *Psycho-Cybernetics*. If you've got other stuff on your mind while you're trying to write your book then you'll be trying to do two things at once. Write all your other thoughts down onto a Do Later list, or if you have an urgent and important job that's playing on your mind then get it done first.

Go on an information diet. This is related to clearing your calculator but if your book requires a research phase you should do this before you start writing. Some find it better not to watch or read the news, read any other books (even fiction) or listen to any instructional audios while writing because once you're in a generative state your mind will automatically try to create connections with everything.

Plan breaks into your writing schedule. This is all about personal style. Joe prefers to write in big spurts of three to four hours non-stop with an hour to recover. Lucy can write in short one to two hour segments, providing the thinking has been done in advance. Others prefer to do it in short sharp blasts of 45 minutes on and 15 off. Experiment until you find the optimal approach for you.

'The art of writing is the art of applying the seat of the pants to the seat of the chair.'
MARY HEATON VORSE

Get the writing habit

When you do feel stuck at the start of a project, your most critical task is to establish a writing schedule. Form the habit of writing at the same time every day (or as regularly as possible), in the same place and with the same routine and props – for instance a specific mug of coffee. The more frequently repeated elements you can get your brain to associate with the act of writing, the more habituated it will become to working creatively on cue.

'Authors with a mortgage never get writers' block.'
MAVIS CHEEK

Along with establishing the habit of regular writing, cultivating the attitude of writing as a job of work, with projects, targets, reviews and deadlines, also militates against the mindset that allows you to get stuck in your book. Most working people do not have the luxury of being unproductive: journalists, speechwriters, business writers and other professional writers would lose their livelihood if they allowed themselves to succumb to writers' block. Think and behave as if you have an external deadline and won't get paid if you don't complete on time.

When you first start writing, stamina may be an issue, and if you can't focus for long periods, your narrative may falter too. The only answer to this is to treat writing as you might an exercise programme: schedule regular short sessions at first, write what comes easily, and slowly build up the quantity and quality of your output. Congratulate yourself on your achievements and don't berate yourself for not achieving your targets. Just keep going and don't give up.

'If you get stuck, get away from your desk. Take a walk, take a bath, go to sleep, make a pie, draw, listen to music, meditate, exercise; whatever you do, don't just stick there scowling at the problem.'
HILARY MANTEL

We won't presume to improve on the words of multi-award-winning Ms Mantel, but will explain that intermittent writers' block can occur when your conscious brain gets overloaded with material – information, options, thoughts, emotions – and won't function creatively until you let it process and file some of this data. Just as sleeping allows the day's experiences to be processed into the subconscious, and you often awake with a solution to a problem that seemed intractable the day before, so a change of activity, especially from mental to physical, gives time and space for writing processing.

Rest and reboot

Some authors swear by the efficacy of a session of vigorous exercise to divert them for sufficient time, and get their re-oxygenated brains firing again. Even stepping away from your screen for long enough to put a load in the washing machine can break the grip of writers' block, and provide a 'reboot' to the creative function. Walking (especially in natural surroundings) and meditation, though, seem especially beneficial to many writers. Both activities, though gently physical, allow the mind to enter a creative state where thoughts and emotions can surface in a free-flowing and seemingly automatic way.

> *'If I don't write to empty my mind, I go mad.'*
> **LORD BYRON**

This is because the conscious mind is limited by what it can hold in short-term memory and the slow progression of rational thought. The subconscious, by contrast, holds a lifetime of experiences and emotions, and makes connections in a far more nimble and esoteric fashion. Writers have to learn to use both mental states: accessing the subconscious for inspiration and working the conscious for the 'perspiration' of book-making. Developing a facility to flip between these states is the long-term cure to writers' block. Being able to combine these states can lead to 'flow' – the ultimate creative state.

But in the short term, and when writers' block strikes out of the blue, take tips from and be inspired by others who have overcome it. They all, essentially, say the same thing:

1. Get started

*'You don't need to wait for inspiration to write.
It's easier to be inspired while writing
than while not writing…'*
JOSIP NOVAKOVICH

'Prescription for writer's block: begin.'
CYNTHIA OZICK

2. Write. Write anything.

'The beautiful part of writing is you don't have to get it right first time, unlike, say, a brain surgeon.'
ROBERT CORMIER

*'Get it down. Take chances. It may be bad but it's
the only way you'll do anything good.'*
WILLIAM FAULKNER

3. Keep writing.

*'A professional writer is an amateur
who didn't quit.'*
RICHARD BACH

Summary

After reading this section, you have a detailed knowledge of how to attack the writing process of your business and self-help book.

You know that finding your own, authentic author voice may take a little time but is vital to your book; and have analysed how to write your book on a chapter-by-chapter basis, with a consistent structure within each chapter.

You've even had a review of grammar and punctuation you might have got a little rusty on since school days.

You have understood that writing a book is a series of discrete tasks that have to be taken step-by-step. The W.R.I.T.E.R. process has separated these out for you: you know how to Write your first draft, and the next section on Editing will take you through the Reviewing, Improving, Testing and Editing (and Repeating where necessary) stages.

4

EDITING YOUR BOOK

'Editing is like pruning the rose bush you thought was so perfect and beautiful until it overgrew the garden.'

LARRY ENRIGHT

As we've described in the W.R.I.T.E.R. process, your book will be much better if you carry out your own rigorous edit before you attempt to get your book professionally edited or published. All traditional publishers and good hybrid publishers will insist on a professional edit before publication, but the better written and polished a manuscript you can present to them, the more respect they will have for you as an author and the less work they will see looming for them.

The R.I.T.E. steps are the most effective method of editing your manuscript.

Review

Finishing the first draft of your business or self-help book is a huge achievement; you should congratulate yourself, then take a break. Start planning, even writing, your next project or turn your attention to something other than your book for a week or so. You should do this, not because the book you've been working on is finished, but because you need to put chronological and emotional distance between you and your book before you can come back and edit it with an objective eye.

Now print out your entire manuscript (on one side of the paper only). A crucial aspect of Reviewing your work is to step outside your writer mode and into reader mode; reading your own words on paper gives you more separation than if you return to them on the screen. You need as much objectivity and distance as possible to identify where there are gaps, repetitions, inconsistencies or actual errors.

Work through your whole book, slowly and carefully, always with a pen in hand. Try, though, to carry out this task at different times to your writing schedule; times when you would normally read books for interest or pleasure.

Don't mistake the step of Reviewing your book for proof reading or editing. This task is not about correcting spelling errors or your grammar (just mark them if you come across any obvious mistakes); it is about assessing whether the structure of your book works; whether your 'story' leads the reader through the information in a logical and compelling way.

As you are reading, make constant notes on your manuscript about your responses.

Be analytical in your approach and make sure that every point you have made in your first draft follows logically from the previous one. If you're not sure, leave a note to remind yourself to try switching paragraphs or sections around when you get back into your electronic version. If your total word count is greater than you planned or wanted, mark up where you can trim or cut elements. If any of your chapters is markedly longer or shorter than the others, look especially hard for ways to reduce or increase their content.

Improve

Switch back into writer mode (and writing schedule) and return to your electronic manuscript with your paper notes by your side. Don't get bogged down in details of spelling or punctuation; take the biggest issues that your Review has highlighted and work on these first.

If you found structural problems, they need to be looked at first: you might have decided that a complete chapter is in the wrong place and needs moving; or sections within one or more of the chapters should be re-ordered. Remember when you do this to check all other references to this aspect of the book, and look at the chapter or section holistically again when you have finished.

Otherwise, sorting out the lesser concerns of filling gaps in content, carrying out additional research, trimming material or sharpening up the presentation of your ideas will clarify the content in your own mind as well as in those of your readers.

Your Review may have shown you that your authorial voice wasn't quite how you want to come across to your readers. Were there places where you became overly technical when you are aiming for a non-professional market? Alternatively, did you over-explain in a way that might seem patronising to a readership well versed in your area of expertise? Although this isn't your final edit, try to improve any areas where your writing voice didn't feel right in your review.

When you've done your best to fix your big picture issues, work through the manuscript from start to finish, correcting every point you've noted from your review, and anything else that shows up as you progress.

Keep an eye out for consistency as you Improve the second draft of your business or self-development book. Ensure that your chapters are all a similar length; that the sections within each chapter are similarly divided up; and that chapters are all structured in the same way.

Test

Now the most important thing you can do is ask a few trusted colleagues to give you their honest opinion. Who should you ask to be a Test reader for your book? Your choice is important and will affect the quality of the feedback you receive. Ideal candidates are:

A professional editor who specialises in your genre of book. If you are planning to get your book professionally edited, now is a good time to get the editor involved. At this stage they could usefully carry out a 'structural edit' and give you broad brush feedback on your structure and writing style. If you follow their advice now, you could save money on the time they need to spend editing your book later.

A colleague or two, who know your subject matter to at least the same depth as you, and can tell you how well you have covered the material, where you have gaps to fill or made any factual errors.

Trusted clients (no more than two) who represent the target market of your business or self-help book, will give you valuable insight into how well you engage your readers and offer them practical solutions to the problems they experience in your niche area.

We suggest you do *not* ask family or friends to act as Test readers at this stage. They will be inclined to give you only the good news, which may be what you would like, but is not what you need to hear. They are unlikely to be your target market and their judgement of your writing will almost certainly be skewed.

For best results, supply your Test readers with an electronic or tidy, printed copy of your manuscript and ask them to make comments on the electronic document or read it with a pen in hand. Be clear with them about what sort of feedback you want from them: it must be honest, specific and constructive, including positive reactions as well as improvements they think you could make. Request politely that they get the job done by an agreed deadline.

Ask them to tell you:

- Their overall reaction – and especially whether they wanted to read on to find out what you were going to say next.
- What they thought the book was going to teach them and whether it lived up to their expectations.
- Whether they were entirely clear about what you were telling them all the time. Ask them to mark sections where they felt lost or confused, and explain why.
- If they found it easy to read – in the sense of not being distracted by poor grammar, spelling, punctuation, hard-to-follow information or instructions (bearing in mind that this is only your first draft).
- If there were any obvious gaps or inconsistencies.
- What they enjoyed most.
- What they would most like you to change.

Accept any negative responses from honest readers at this stage as a gift; they may save you from rejection by agents or publishers, or bad reviews from critics or paying readers.

Edit

Only at this point, with notes and critiques from your Test readers and possibly a professional editor, will you have an idea of the size and complexity of your editing task. You should expect it to be as long or big a project as the initial writing. Whether your structure hangs together, but your style and grammar need a careful edit; or you realise that an overhaul of some sections is required, don't be daunted.

First collate all your feedback. It might not all be consistent; your readers may disagree with each other and take different points of view. Take seriously anything that two or more of readers do agree on. Try to assess criticism objectively, even though you would rather listen to the praise. Decide which suggestions you are going to accept and implement.

Be systematic

While everyone should work in the way that best suits their methods and thought processes, it is crucial to be systematic when editing. This means stepping back from your investment in all aspects of your book and looking for what might be missing such as a crucial step, a case study or a key piece of information in the right place. Focus on cutting out distractions. Is there too much personal opinion or too much focus on your own experience? Are the quotes and case studies furthering your message or getting in the way? Be systematic – and ruthless.

'Put down everything that comes into your head and then you're a writer. But an author is one who can judge his own stuff's worth, without pity, and destroy most of it.'
COLETTE

Big picture, then the detail

Once you have finessed your book in terms of the wider issues, it's time to edit the manuscript for fine detail. If you have made some major revisions and done some extensive rewriting, it could be helpful to take another break before you start the close work on syntax and style.

In addition to checking against the information in the sections on paragraph and sentence construction, as well as grammar and punctuation, make sure you:

- Check your facts – dates, science, events, places or people...
- Vary your vocabulary – try not to use the same word more than once in a paragraph, let alone a sentence; find different ways to express yourself.
- Make each sentence and every word count – shorten, delete and rephrase for accuracy and simplicity (more on this shortly).
- Read aloud for rhythm – if any sentence doesn't feel quite right, read it aloud to discover where it's losing pace or tying itself in knots.
- Get up to speed with grammar – if you're not already a grammar nerd, buy one, or more, handbooks on grammar and punctuation and look up anything you're not sure of. Learn the rules and remember to apply them: it's slow going at first, but it will improve your writing – and editing – immeasurably. Clarity of expression leads to clarity of thought.

'Edit your manuscript until your fingers bleed and you have memorized every last word. Then, when you are certain you are on the verge of insanity... edit one more time!'

C.K. WEBB

Repeat

The final R in the W.R.I.T.E.R. process is for Repeat. When you reach the end of the self-editing process, re-read, ask others to read and give feedback. Repeat the process if necessary – as many times as required. When you have come to the end of your own editing abilities, seriously consider paying a professional editor to review and polish your manuscript, even if you are going to submit to an agent or traditional publisher. As any successful author knows, whether you are going to self-publish your book, or try to get it traditionally published, quality editing is worth the investment.

Tighter Writing

If there's one thing that divides the amateur from the professional writer, it's the tautness of their prose style. Amateur writers' sentences often meander, twist and turn; they use many more words than required; and over-complicate their syntax in an effort to sound sophisticated. This can end up confusing readers, as well as slowing down the progression of their book. An agent or commissioning editor will reject a manuscript with such a writing style before they reach the bottom of the first page.

> *'To write well, express yourself like the common people, but think like a wise man.'*
> ARISTOTLE

Seasoned writers, on the other hand, create crisp, elegant sentences in which every single word is precise and necessary, which have correct grammar and functional punctuation. They will make sure, through several drafts, rewrites and self-edits, that each phrase delivers its message with the fewest and the simplest, though most appropriate, words. This makes their writing easy to read and dense with meaning – a fully satisfying experience.

What is Loose Writing?

While tight writing is so well-honed that you could not remove or change a single word without altering the meaning or spoiling the rhythm, loose writing is full of extra and unnecessary articles, repetition, passive verbs, woolly words and wordy phrases. If you try to read loose writing aloud, it will be hard to make sense of sentences, to find a good rhythm or to emphasise the right words.

This is not something you need to worry about in your first draft. If getting your message out fast and furiously is the best way for you, do it. You can come back and tighten up the style in a second, third or fourth draft – as in the

W.R.I.T.E.R. process. Getting every paragraph, sentence and phrase concise and precise is hard work, and may take longer than writing the book in the first place.

Four Tighter Writing Tips

Here are four questions to check against every sentence as you revise:

1. Have you used the simplest word?

It's easy when we write to try and be too clever, to imagine that a short, everyday word isn't good enough for the readers of our business or self-help book. We can make the mistake of picking fancy, longer words which are less accurate and distract from the flow. Choose the shortest, simplest word which will do the job, and reserve the longer, more obscure ones for when you really need them.

Use *so* rather than *accordingly; begin* or *start* are better than *commence; size* is at least as good as *magnitude;* and please, never use words like *sub-optimal* instead of *worse.*

2. Is every word necessary?

We are lax about language when we talk and our instinct is often to write as we speak, packing in our usual excess verbiage, even if not the ums, ers and 'you know what I means'. Examine each sentence and eliminate every unnecessary word; combine sentences to remove repetition and to make the writing dense; divide a long, rambling sentence into two or three more compact ones.

Imagine trimming the rough edges off your sentences with a nice, sharp knife until you've got a beautifully honed piece of wood. Try whittling some typically overused phrases down to a single word, like these:

Are in possession of (have); at this point in time (now); is able to (can); in spite of the fact that (although); in the not too distant future (soon); on a weekly basis (weekly); in the vicinity of (near);

3. Are your verbs active and direct?

The active voice is almost always simpler and shorter than the passive; it also tends to be a less pretentious way of constructing a sentence.

The marketing plan was devised and the advertisements were placed by the agency is longer and more pompous than *The agency devised the marketing plan and placed the advertisements.*

Be wary of sentences containing 'There are/were/is/was...' and '...who were/are/was/is...'. These introductory and descriptive phrases are usually redundant. Rather than *There were some errors in the plan which caused the marketing to be less effective as it was rolled out*, write *Errors in the marketing plan caused the roll out to be less effective.*

4. Can you cut out adverbs, adjectives and qualifiers?

> *'The road to hell is paved with adverbs.'*
> **STEPHEN KING**

Adverbs rarely add value to a sentence. If you need to add impact to a weak verb, choose a stronger verb and ditch the adverb. Rather than, *I effectively promoted my book by enthusiastically talking about it on stage*, write *I sold my book through public speaking*. This is also a way of ensuring you choose the most accurate wording.

Mark Twain said it all – and with commendable brevity – about adjectives:

> *'As to the adjective, when in doubt, strike it out.'*

He also made a similar point about qualifiers – very, rather, quite, some, etc:

> *'Substitute 'damn' every time you're inclined to write 'very': your editor will delete it and the writing will be just as it should be.'*
> **MARK TWAIN**

Style rules: consistency and standards

This short checklist is based on our own brief for editors. You may want to make your own rules but this will at least point you toward some of the things you need to make consistent.

We suggest you become familiar with Hart's Rules which can be found in the *Oxford Guide To Style* or if you're using International (US) English you can read *The Chicago Manual of Style.*

- **Consistency** – spellings, hyphens, punctuation, formatting and spacing should be applied consistently throughout the document.
- **Chapter headings** numbered 1, 2, 3 etc. Not Chapter One, just 1 where needed.
- **Sub-headings** made compelling (like a headline) or instructive (clear what's included) as appropriate. Be consistent.
- **Chapter structure** is consistent, with each chapter having same sub sections e.g. Introduction, Examples, Summary etc. for every chapter.
- **Format heading levels** using Heading 1, Heading 2, Heading 3 etc.
- **Format body text** as 'Normal' and use only italics and bold as appropriate for emphasis.
- **Capitals** – do not use for stress; only use for acronyms and to begin the title of people or things. To stress a word in a sentence use italics not capitals.
- **Italics** is only for foreign words, stress and titles of books, films, plays, albums etc. (The names of songs, poems, articles should not be italic, but within inverted commas.)
- **Bold** can be used to introduce points in bullet lists as used here.
- **Hyphens** – use sparingly but almost always use for words that begin with anti, non and neo and to avoid

ambiguities e.g. 'a little-used car' versus 'a little used-car'.

- **Leader dots** – are a special typographic character and should consist of just 3 dots and no more: … is acceptable; ………… is not.
- **Exclamations and Questions** – only ever use one punctuation point e.g. … – ? not ??? – Do not mix – ?.? is unacceptable. If you must add an exclamation to a question then the question mark should always come first e.g. ?!
- **New paragraphs** should be separated by a line break fully left aligned with no indent.
- **New sentences** should have single spaces (not double or triple) after punctuation for previous sentence.
- **Speech** – begin with single inverted commas e.g. 'The publisher told me, "always use single inverted commas first for our titles", so I do.'
- **Jargon, acronyms, abbreviations** – explain/define any jargon word or acronym when it's first used and use shortcut afterwards. Don't put full stops in an acronym, e.g. use NATO not N.A.T.O.
- **Short Words** should be used in place of long ones where sensible because they are easy to spell and easy to understand. In general, it's preferable to use: 'about' to 'approximately' – 'after' to 'following' – 'let' to 'permit' – 'but' to 'however' – 'use' to 'utilise' – 'make' to 'manufacture' – 'take part' to 'participate' – 'set up' to 'establish' – 'enough' to 'sufficient' – 'show' to 'demonstrate' – 'help' to 'assistance' – 'find out' to 'ascertain' etc.

- **Fluff Words** should be removed where practical. See how it reads if you shorten words e.g. 'track record' to 'record' – 'weather conditions' to 'weather' – 'large-scale' to 'large' – 'this time around' to 'this time' – 'free of charge' to 'free' – 'safe haven' to 'haven' – 'most probably' to 'probably' etc.
- **Very** – if this word occurs in a sentence then try removing it to see if the meaning is changed. 'The omens are good' may be more powerful than 'The omens are very good'. Never use 'very, very'.
- **Spelling** – if your main market is in Britain, use UK English – 'ise/isation' not 'ize/ization' – 'labour' not 'labor' – 'colour' not 'color'. Also use 'while' not 'whilst' – 'amid' not 'amidst' etc.
- **Active voice** is preferred over the passive voice. 'The book was written by her' is better as 'She wrote the book'.
- **Sentences** should be short and punchy not long and meandering. Simplify long expressions where possible e.g. 'now' is better than 'at this moment in time' – 'if' is better than 'in the event that' etc.
- **Dates** – use dd-mm-yyyy or, to avoid ambiguity entirely, Day Month Year.

Summary

This section has taken you through the Review, Improve, Test and Edit (and Repeat as necessary) steps of the W.R.I.T.E.R. process, helping you to polish and edit the first draft of your business or self-help book to a high level.

You also understand how a professional editor looks at tighter writing and consistency in style and formatting; if you can do some of this work yourself you will save your editor time, yourself money and impress any potential publisher with your professionalism.

You have a comprehensive system for editing your manuscript before you start the process of getting your business or self-help book published. Let's move onto that now.

Publishing Your Book

5

GETTING YOUR BOOK PUBLISHED

I've got a traditional publishing contract now, but it doesn't stop me from self-publishing... There is no need to go down one avenue and not the other these days, you can do both... It doesn't really matter anymore how you go about achieving that as long as two things happen: you get your book read by as many people as possible and you get paid for writing it.

NICK SPALDING

Many first-time authors have stumbled here, with the result that all their hard work simply sits gathering dust.

The fact is, to the chagrin of many traditional publishers and some of their authors, there is no longer any barrier to getting your book in print and selling via the same channels as the big publishers. Just because the barriers are down, though, it doesn't necessarily mean the road is easy. The good news is that by the time you've finished this chapter you'll know exactly what your publishing options are and how to choose the one that will serve you best.

There are currently three clear paths to getting a business or self-help book published:

- Traditional/legacy publishing
- Self-publishing
- Hybrid/supported publishing

Let's look in detail at each option…

The Traditional Publisher

Traditional publishers include the big name, international publishers that everyone has heard of, often known as 'The Big Five' (depending on who has taken over whom lately). Each one owns a range of imprints devoted to different types of fiction and nonfiction, including business or self-help, books. There are also a wide range of smaller, independent traditional publishers, often with their own niche in nonfiction and business or self-help publishing.

The 'traditional' publishing business model is for the publisher to contract the author to publish their book. The contract may include the publisher buying the copyright of the author's intellectual property for a defined period of time, which may limit the author's freedom to use their material for other purposes. The publisher may – though this is a diminishing practice – pay the author an 'advance': money in advance of publication that will be recouped by the publisher from the author's royalties from sales. Many authors never actually earn their advance back – in other words the only money they ever see is the advance – which, unless they are a famous author or celebrity, on an hourly rate of payment for their work is probably lower than the minimum wage. Paying advances which are not recouped are simply a massive financial drain for traditional publishers, so increasingly only big name authors are receiving them.

A big traditional publisher is likely to pay an author 8% to 10% of net receipts from sales of their book (after production, printing and distribution costs, and less the discount payable to wholesalers and retailers); this can be as little as 20p from the sale of an average-priced book. Smaller publishers, especially those who only use print-on-demand distribution (more on this shortly), may pay a higher royalty. Bookshaker, which operates as a traditional publisher, pays a generous 20% of net receipts royalty.

The traditional publisher then takes all the financial responsibility for getting the book published, including usually: editing, design, typeset, cover design and printing. Traditional publishers, as well as publishing through online retailers like Amazon, will probably produce an 'up front' print run (usually between 1,000 and 3,000 copies – or more if you're an established author with a sales track record) of the book, and distribute it through physical bookstores. This, however, is becoming increasingly expensive and is often only profitable for well-known authors or other best-sellers where publishers can invest in in-store merchandising (either paying for this directly or offering a huge discount). The bigger publishers can use their high selling books to subsidise the distribution of new authors, but smaller traditional publishers may choose not to risk the funding print and distribution costs of a new author's book.

Distributing a book through online retailers is often done through 'print-on-demand'. This is a different and comparatively new printing process through which very small print runs (as low as one copy at a time) can be produced at a reasonable price, as they are ordered by purchasers. It is true that the quality of print-on-demand (POD) books is slightly lower than offset litho (traditional) printed books, but POD technology and costs are improving all the time. POD allows publishers to avoid risking money on printing books in advance of sales and cuts down the risk of having unsold stock returned or pulped.

Apart from the cost of print, storage and shipping, selling books through physical bookstores is often unprofitable for publishers, and therefore authors, because retailers mainly insist on stocking titles on 'sale or return'. Any unsold books will not be paid for, and must be returned to the publisher at their own expense, or simply destroyed. Mainstream publishers typically give a book three months in bookstores before giving up hope of making further sales. If the book doesn't perform well they abandon the marketing and distribution to focus on new titles and the author's book ends up being sold for pennies (often less than the physical cost to produce it) in remainders stores such as The Works.

Although landing a big name publishing contract is often the dream for many aspiring authors, being published with a mainstream traditional publisher is not for everyone.

The pros of traditional publishing

Kudos: For many authors the cachet of being taken on by a well-known publishing house is key to their strategy (and ego), and with such a publisher's backing this can translate into a higher media profile, higher fees and a better shot at fame.

Distribution: Your book (at least for a limited time) is more likely to find its way onto more bookstores' shelves than other publishing options allow. Although being on a shelf in a bookshop amongst loads of other books is no guarantee of success (especially as more and more sales are going online) it is likely you will make more actual sales (though not necessarily more profit).

Marketing: All big, and some small, traditional publishers have in-house marketing and publicity departments, which are there to support authors. In our experience, the efficacy of these departments is questionable, and without incredible luck any business or self-help book will require the author to work hard at promotion (of themselves and their book) to be a success.

Focus: A traditional publisher takes on the project management of getting your book published, allowing you to concentrate on the main job of writing your next book.

Risk Aversion: If you're risk averse or don't have money to spare, a traditional publishing contract with a proper publisher means you won't have to spend any money on the production of your book – and if you're lucky or famous, they may even give you an advance. (However, given the level of competition for publishing contracts, many authors choose to pay for a professional edit *before* submitting their manuscript to an agent or publisher.)

The cons of traditional publishing

Loss of Freedom: When you work for a publisher (because that's what your contract will mean), some of your creative freedom and your freedom of speech will be quelled. They will need to ensure your book fits their brand and they'll have their own (often good, though sometimes not) ideas about how the book should look, what it will be called, what it should be about and how it should be positioned. Many contracts will also include a clause in the contract saying how long you've got to complete your manuscript. Failing to meet the deadlines imposed by your publisher can result in you losing your contract and your advance.

Loss of Control: What you can do with your book (or even say about your book) will be limited. You may need to get approval for a marketing or advertising campaign you'd like to run and your ability to write another book with another publisher (or even to self-publish) may be subject to certain conditions in your contract. You may think you're only signing over rights to one book but you could end up signing over your future work too.

Loss of Ownership: Many large publishers will stipulate that they own the rights to your work in other languages, territories and formats. Be careful what you're signing and ensure you know your rights. You could end up watching your publisher get rich while you remain unrewarded.

Lack of Marketing: The average mainstream publisher organises distribution, puts your book in their catalogue and puts out a press release. These days, as an author, and whichever way you publish your book, marketing and promotion is 100% your job. Even if you're a big name celebrity or you have just come off the back of a best-seller (which you will have had to work hard to promote), your publisher still won't be able to do the interviews or your social media for you. You have to be the spokesperson for your book and that means you're going to need to hustle and be adept at social media.

Loss of Profit: As the publisher has taken all the financial risk to get your book published, you will be paid the 'mouse's share' of the proceeds from your book sales. If you have used an agent (often the only way to get into a big publisher), you will have to give 10% to 15% of your income to them. In fact, the publisher will pay your agent, who will pay you after they've taken their fee. Trying to land a good agent can be just as difficult as landing a publishing deal. Agents add an additional layer of time, control and cost to your publication.

Loss of Time and Opportunity: Until you start selling books the whole process is still a 'cost-money' exercise; you could spend more money and time chasing a publishing contract or agent than if you just self-published, and in the gap, who knows how many opportunities you may have missed.

Lack of Speed: Publishing behemoths are full of really talented people, but the organisations themselves are slow, cumbersome and full of political, financial and shareholder pressures. This all leads to a long delay between landing a deal and selling any books. In addition to the time spent courting and signing with a traditional publisher, it ttypically takes a year from delivering your manuscript for your book to be out and selling.

Self-Publishing

> *'Today, authors are in the idea-making business, not the book business. In short, this means that publishing a book is less about sales and much more about creating a brand. The real customers of books are no longer just readers but now include speaking agents, CEOs, investors, and startups.'*
>
> **RYAN HOLIDAY, AUTHOR** *TRUST ME, I'M LYING*

Many self-publishers do so, not as a last resort, but because they worked out the income they could make without the traditional publishers taking the lion's share of the profit. The fact is, even a complete publishing newbie with awful distribution can still make more money by self-publishing than by going mainstream.

Self-publishing can look like an attractive publishing option financially, but if you are not technically knowledgeable, prepared to put in a lot of time learning how to, or pay other freelance individuals to assist you, you will need to think carefully about this option.

The pros of self-publishing

Freedom, Control and Ownership: Your book is your own and no publisher can tell you what they want in it, how it should look and where it should be positioned. You can do whatever you like with your own material: write it as you want it to appear, repackage it in different formats, give some away free...

Maximum Profit: All the financial risk in getting your book published has been yours, the work in getting it distributed has been yours, so 100% of your sales income comes directly to you.

Time and Opportunity: You are working to your own timescales: on the one hand you have no deadlines, unless you set them yourself; on the other, you are not waiting on other people's input and schedules. You can take as long or as short a time as you like to write, get the other aspects of publishing sorted out, and spend as much or as little time as you choose on marketing and promotion.

Low Risk: You can spend virtually nothing (though professional editing and cover design is strongly advised) except your own time on preparing your own book for self-publishing.

The cons of self-publishing

Lower Kudos: In some areas there is still lower status in a self-published book, especially if your book appears amateurish in its content or production values. For instance, it will be hard, if not impossible, to get your book reviewed in the mainstream media.

Distribution: You will not be able to get as comprehensive a listing with wholesalers, who service physical bookstores, if you are not a 'publisher' with a list of at least ten books and additional subscriptions to their services.

Project Management: Unless you pay someone else to manage the process for you, every aspect of the publication of your book is down to you. If you want to involve professionals like editors and designers, you will need to source them, manage and co-ordinate their input, and also learn the technical side of book production, publishing, distribution and marketing.

Lack of Marketing: Even more than working with any kind of publisher, as a self-published author, marketing and promotion is 110% your job. You have to be the social marketer, PR agent and spokesperson for your book and that means you're going to need to spend time hustling.

Hidden costs: It is possible to self-publish an e-book for almost no cost to you, but to publish a printed book means you have to buy a minimum of ten ISBN numbers at the very least. To produce a professional looking e- and print book, you will really need to pay an editor and cover designer; a typesetter will also make the 'inner' of your book look better and more readable than you can; and converting a professional typeset to various e-book formats might also involve a skilled professional.

Technical know-how: In addition to all the know-how required to self-publish, including buying ISBNs, choosing print-on-demand or print-then-sell approaches, billing and accounting, you will also need many, often disparate skills, such as editing, graphic design, typesetting, proof-reading etc. Unless you have all these skills, the only way to do a good job is to pay experts. This increases your outlay and, as you're ultimately responsible for every aspect of the final product, means if you get it wrong you may have to pay again. It's not unheard of for self-publishing projects to go way over budget when you take a piecemeal approach to getting the job done.

Post Publication Hassle: Deciding to self-publish essentially means you're taking the decision to become a publisher. This business involves additional hassles including invoicing, chasing payment, sending books for legal deposit (a legal requirement in the UK), shipping to distributors or customers, specific publishing insurance, collating royalty information for tax purposes and much more.

Hybrid Publishing

'I believe you're going to see more partnerships between publishers and self-publishing and… that you're going to see publishers start to adopt the partnership model that self-publishing brings with it.'
PENNY SANSEVIERI, HUFFINGTON POST

There are many terms out there, at the time of writing, for the kind of publishing that offers a bridge between traditional publishing and self-publishing: supported publishing, paid-for publishing, subsidised publishing, partnership publishing... The industry, and its authors, seem to be converging on the term 'hybrid publishing' to describe a publishing contract where the author pays upfront for the costs associated with producing their book – such as editing, typesetting, cover design, ISBN, print distribution, eBook conversion and distribution, royalty collection/calculation, and ongoing trouble-shooting – and in return for their reduced financial risk, whilst getting some return for their project management of the book, the publisher pays the author a more generous royalty than they would receive through traditional publishing.

This is what we do at Rethink Press, which we founded after finding that Bookshaker had to turn down too many well written and interesting business or self-help books. We liked many of the books offered, but considered the markets too small for us to ensure a break-even, let alone return on investment. Others simply fell outside the areas we had defined for the Bookshaker imprint, although they deserved publication. We canvassed some of our authors and found that many were prepared to pay for author services in order to get their books published by reputable professionals, under the imprint of a publisher, rather than present a self-published book to the world, and were happy to take a higher royalty in return for their input.

These authors, and others who have published with Rethink Press and other hybrid publishers, did not want to jump through the hoops of chasing a traditional publishing contract – with the uncertainty of gaining a positive result and the inevitable delays even if they did. Neither did they wish to learn, nor spend time getting to grips with, the technicalities of publishing for themselves; nor source and manage the range of individual professionals whose input they would otherwise need. They wanted their books published professionally in a short time-frame to underpin their platform of niche expertise, and to work with publishing industry experts, enabling them to get on with developing their core business.

> *'Call it a business card, a resume, a billboard, or whatever you choose, but the short of it is that books are no longer just books. They are branding devices and credibility signals.'*
> RYAN HOLIDAY

One problem with hybrid publishing is that, in some circles, it has been tarred with the brush of the legacy practice of 'vanity publishing'. Before the advent of print-on-demand and online booksellers, anyone who wanted to publish their own book had to do it using so-called vanity publishers. These companies made a portion of their money by persuading hapless authors, often of autobiographies and personal memoirs as well as information books, to pay for big print runs of their book. They would then have to store sometimes thousands of these volumes, with no means of distributing them other than gifts/sales to family and friends, or paid advertising. Unsurprisingly, vanity publishers earned themselves a bad name (literally) and a bad reputation. Traditionally published authors looked down on self-published authors as not having written a good enough book to be accepted by a 'real' publisher.

With self-published books, in print and e-book format, now selling as many as traditionally published books, this is (mostly) no longer the case. In fact, the tables may turn so that traditionally published authors are seen by people who embrace the new way as old-fashioned and lacking the entrepreneurship and means to publish their own books.

Reputable hybrid publishing companies should be entirely transparent about their costs and contracts, and provide authors with only the services they need and want. There are some large (and possibly some small) 'self-publishing companies' (a misnomer and contradictory term) that continue the ethos of the original vanity publishers: make money at all costs, especially at the author's cost, any and every which way you can. This can involve providing poor services at high cost, over-selling and under-performing, selling services such as marketing and promotion as certain ways to sell books, which are rarely justified. Some of these 'self-publishing' giants, despite their poor reputations, have recently been bought up by big traditional publishers, apparently in order for the latter to cash in on the new publishing business model. Authors are told that if their book does well under the 'self-publishing' imprint, they have a chance of being published by the traditional imprint. We have yet to hear of a transfer of this kind.

Authors should always check out hybrid publishers (publishers whom they are going to pay for services) before working with them. Look up any candidates on the Editors and Predators website, http://pred-ed.com/; search 'disputes with (name of company)' or 'problems with (name of company)' and see what comes up; try to find at least one author who has worked with the company, if it hasn't been recommended to you by one. Make sure you talk to the main person you will be working with; the person responsible for project-managing your book. If they can't or don't answer any questions to your satisfaction, beware. Similarly, if they try to up-sell you anything you didn't plan, want, need or budget for, look elsewhere.

Similarly, check the contract you are offered by a hybrid publisher with great care. At Rethink Press our contracts are for the non-exclusive right to publish your work in book form in the English language for five years. We do not take control of your intellectual property or restrict your ability to use your own material in other ways. If you wanted to end the contract early for almost any reason, we would release you from it, believing that an unhappy author or negative relationship is not working for either party. Some authors who have published with big 'self-publishing' companies have found themselves unable to get released from contracts they thought they had flexibility with.

Pros of hybrid publishing

Freedom, Control and Ownership: Your book is your own and a reputable hybrid publisher will work with you to make your book exactly how you want and need it to be, in content, look and positioning. As long as you don't drastically change your book during production you will know in advance how much you are paying. This is much harder to do if you're managing your own team of freelancers/suppliers.

Professional Production: The editor, designers, typesetter will be experienced, used to working with authors such as you, and with each other. You will not have to source the professional contributors to your book, and with their input your book will have a professional look and feel.

Project Management: As well as not having to search for the right professionals to create your book, the time-consuming and intensive task of managing them will be done by an experienced publisher, leaving you free to start marketing, working on your core business, and/or writing your next book. They will also manage your royalties, deal with queries and issues post-publication.

A Real Publisher: Although there is decreasing stigma about self-publishing, your book will have all the benefits of being produced and branded by a real publishing company. Like a traditional publisher, hybrid publishers have existing accounts with Amazon, other booksellers and wholesalers.

Quality: If you choose well, you can be assured the end product is high quality and professional. The typeset, design and quality of your content should be top-notch.

High royalties: As you have taken a lot of the upfront risk of publishing your book, your hybrid publisher should be paying you higher royalties. At Rethink Press we pay authors a royalty of 60% of net profit.

Easy access to stock: A good hybrid publisher will be transparent about costs should you wish to order author copies to sell direct. Because they're almost certainly using print on demand it's possible to order very small or very large quantities at a decent price. This means you only need to keep stock of a small quantity of books and you can top up stock at any time.

Cons of hybrid publishing

Financial risk: There are hybrid publishers with packages to suit most pockets, but the author will always have to pay some upfront costs to get published. This means until you've sold enough copies to break even on your investment you're out of pocket.

Lack of Marketing: Hybrid publishers may be able to offer (paid for) marketing support, but as with self-publishing, marketing and promotion is your job. You have to be the social marketer, PR agent and spokesperson for your book and that means you're going to need to spend time to get sales results.

Distribution: Although your book may be listed with the wholesalers from whom physical bookstores order stock, it is less likely to find its way onto many bookstores' shelves unless it is your supportive local or specialist bookstore, or a customer orders your book through a bookshop.

Predators: There are 'self-publishing' companies who regularly take money from first-time authors, deliver poor services, publish low quality books and badger their clients with up-selling offers for additional services, some of which – like marketing or PR packages – deliver no value. All authors should check out any potential hybrid publishing company before they sign contracts with or pay money to them.

Formatting your manuscript

Ensuring your manuscript is correctly formatted is essential if you are going to submit it to an agent, publisher or editor. Why? Because it makes your work easier to read, to assess, to mark up and, in due course, to typeset. Additionally, because there are publishing industry standards which, if you appear ignorant of them, or choose to ignore them, make you look unprofessional, unhelpful and reduce your chances of being considered as a serious author.

The guidelines we're going to give you are the basic formatting rules for business or self-help book manuscripts, but many agents and publishers have their own specific requirements which they make clear on their websites or in publicity material, usually as 'Submission Guidelines'. The first rule is to find, read and follow those Submission

Guidelines – do not make the mistake of thinking it won't matter if you don't, or your own formatting ideas are better. You may well have to make changes, large or small, to your manuscript for each organisation you submit it to. If you want to get a foot in the door with them – just do it!

Microsoft Word is the publishing industry's default software for reading and editing book manuscripts. If you are a Mac user, it would be sensible to invest in the full Word for Mac package as without it you may not be able to read your editor's inline markup or marginal notes.

Font

Use only one font (typeface) throughout, for all body text and headings too. Stick to a common, much used font rather than something you consider more attractive or original. If you're sending a manuscript electronically, you want to be sure the recipient has the same font on their computer, or your formatting may appear wrong to them. The two safest are Times New Roman, a serif font which some publishers prefer; and Arial, the most commonly used sans-serif typeface. Whichever one you use, stick to it – don't try to get creative by putting some sections in a different font, or trying to represent, say, handwriting with a cursive font. This is a job for a designer/typesetter, not the author.

When you are writing case studies or breakout boxes *do not* put them in text boxes or coloured (even grey) background boxes. Just indicate where they start and finish and let the designer/typesetter create the look. All your boxes and formatting will have to be removed – and actually make your manuscript look amateurish, rather than the opposite.

Whichever font you choose, the size should be 12pt and black throughout. Make headings **bold,** and emphases, titles and non-English words *italic* (do *not* underline – this editing convention was used in written or typewritten manuscripts to indicate what should be italicised in typeset). Do this by highlighting and using the tabs for bold and italic; do *not* change the typeface to, for instance, 'Arial Bold' or 'Times New Roman Italic'. Do not use CAPITALS for emphasis – or ***bold italics***, come to that.

Margins, spacing and indentation

Margins should be one inch all around the page (this is the default margins setting for MS Word).

Line-spacing should be 1.5 (especially if your manuscript is very long) or double-spaced. (Synopses, though, are single-spaced so you can get them onto one page.)

Paragraphs should *either* have two line returns between them, *or* start the first line with a 0.5 inch indent, but not both. If you choose to indent paragraphs, the opening paragraph of a chapter or section should not be indented. Indents should be created with a tab, not by pressing the space bar several times. As editors and publishers, we personally prefer non-indented paragraphs with a double space between them as they are easier to mark-up and make less work for a typesetter.

Full stops/periods should be followed by one space only – not two. Older writers, who learned on a typewriter, may have been taught to put two blank spaces after a full stop. This is no longer needed on computers, which produce more accurately spaced documents, and is not correct in manuscripts today.

Line breaks should only be made at the end of paragraphs; don't put in any hard returns in the middle of paragraphs to make a line end neatly. The whole shape and look of the manuscript will change in typeset and any interventions like this on your part will create extra work for the typesetter.

First page, headers and footers

On your cover page, which should have single line spacing, put your name and contact info on the upper left hand side of the page; genre and word count (rounded to the nearest thousand) on the upper right (both single-spaced). If you are represented by an agent, the contact details should be theirs.

Your title, centred and in capitals, goes a third of the way down the page; two lines below put 'by,' and two lines below that, your name.

From the second page – the start of your book – you should be in double or 1.5 line spacing.

Chapter/section headings should be in bold and can either be centred or justified to the left. The body text should be justified to the left only, leaving it 'ragged' on the right hand side. Chapters should start on a new page, but there is no need to leave a blank page between chapters.

The Header should start on the second page of your manuscript and should consist of, on the left, your title (or part of it, if it's very long) followed by a slash and your surname; on the right, the page number (starting from '1' on the second page).

The Footer can be used for a copyright assertion, best in a smaller font (8pt – 10pt), such as: *How To Write Your Book Without The Fuss* © Joe Gregory & Lucy McCarraher, January 2015. (The copyright sign is produced in Word by typing (c) with no spaces.)

Dots and dashes...

Dots, or ellipsis, as they are really called, which indicate an unfinished thought or, at the end of a sentence, a trailing off into silence... should be formatted like that. Three (no more) dots immediately after the last word, with a space before the next word.

Dashes come in two forms: en-dashes (approx the width of a letter 'n') are the short ones used to hyphenate two words; em-dashes (approx the width of an 'm') are the longer ones often used in place of brackets or to indicate speech has been broken off. (Create an em-dash in Word by typing an en-dash, immediately followed by a hard return, then a backspace to return to the end of the now longer dash.) An oft-asked question is, should there or should there not be spaces around em-dashes? In the US there is more of a preference for no spaces — like this. But in the UK, always have a space before and after an em-dash — like that.

Quotation marks (inverted commas) come in doubles or singles for speech and quotation. The modern preference is to use singles, 'like this', with doubles for quotes "within" quotes. Italicise (without quotation marks) the titles of books, newspapers, journals, albums and TV shows, but not the titles of songs, poems or articles, which should be unitalicised in quotation marks. Actual quotations of no more than two or three lines go within quotation marks as part of a paragraph; longer quotations form a separate, indented paragraph without quotation marks.

Numbers from one to nine are generally written in letters, while those from 10 upwards go in numerals. The editor's industry bible, *Hart's Rules,* also allows for numbers one to ninety-nine to be written in letters, with numerals used for 100 and above. Whichever you choose, be consistent. Speaking of which…

Consistency

Above all, be consistent in your formatting, spelling and grammar. If you are unsure of a correct, or whether to use a UK or US, spelling, make a decision and stick with it. Don't write 'OK' sometimes, 'ok' at other times, and 'okay' occasionally. Similarly, don't use double quotation marks around some dialogue and singles around others – unless you have a typographical reason to do so. Nothing drives an editor madder! Again, it makes you look unprofessional and as if you haven't bothered to consider such things.

Submitting Your Manuscript

Your business or self-help book is the best you can make it; your manuscript is clean and professional; if you are looking for a traditional, or even hybrid, publisher, you are now ready to make your submissions.

To find an appropriate traditional publisher, buy *The Writer's And Artist's Yearbook* (*www.writersandartists.co.uk*) and shortlist publishers you'd like to work with. Even if they say they only accept submissions from agents it's worth sending a quick email or letter to check. If they really only consider submissions through agents, try other publishers first.

Find out what a publisher's submission guidelines are and follow these to the letter to present your detailed synopsis, but ignore their rules about not chasing up (as long as you do it in a friendly and assertive way). Still, you should give them plenty of time because they really do have to deal with loads of enquiries just like yours. Ignore the old etiquette of only offering your book to one publisher at a time; instead choose your top five publishers and send your synopsis to all of them. If you end up in the fortunate position of having two or more publishers interested you can play them off against each other.

Submitting your manuscript to agents who can represent you to publishers, or directly to publishers, is known as a 'query'. To accompany your book you will need to prepare two sales pitches: your synopsis and covering letter. Both these one-page items need to be crafted with care and precision; they are your book's introduction to a wider audience and if they don't announce you as an excellent writer and pique the professional reader's interest in your manuscript, you will have done yourself and your business or self-help message a disservice.

Covering letter

Your covering letter should fit on a single page and follow this simple, three-paragraph format.

Salutation: write to the specific person you have identified – it's your call as to whether you address them by their first name, Ms/Mr... or, safest, both names.

Paragraph 1: introduce and summarise your business or self-help book (subject and format and no more than two sentences of description). Mention why you are submitting to this agent/publisher (You represent author a and author b, whose books xxx and yyy attract a similar readership to mine/have influenced my writing ...). If you have spoken to someone in their organisation, you can mention their name and say they advised you to write to this person.

Paragraph 2: Introduce yourself as an author. You might want to say what your current employment is, especially if relevant to the subject matter. Explain why you are 'qualified' to write your book (either formal qualifications or personal experience of subject matter); be imaginative and persuasive. *Don't* talk about aspects of your life unrelated to the book (amateur pianist, mother of three). Give details of your writing background – especially any articles you've had published online or in print, or industry awards or recognition. Do *not* quote family or friends who love your writing or subject matter.

Paragraph 3: Thank them for reading your work, tell them you look forward to hearing from them and give contact details – phone numbers, email address – where they can reach you and, if appropriate, a website and other online presence where they can learn more about you.

Your business or self-help book synopsis

You'll often need to rework this to fit an individual publisher's requirements, but your basic synopsis should answer the following questions (once you've worked through the other sections of this book you should be able to answer these questions easily and confidently):

> **Market/Audience:** Who will want the book and why will it appeal to them? Why do you think the topic of your book is hot right now? What evidence do you have? What's the anticipated market size?

> **Big Promise/Big Idea:** What's the big promise or your big idea? Is your book contentious or ground-breaking in some way? What's your book's 'wow factor'?

> **Impact:** What will your book do for the reader and how

will they behave, think or feel differently? How will things be better for them after reading your book?

Style: Is your book informal or formal? Academic or experiential? Practical or theoretical? How-to or inspirational? Will it shock? Will it inform? Will it encourage and inspire?

Endorsements: Have you got a suitable big name to write your Foreword? Do you have any praise or fans already?

Author: Why are you uniquely positioned to write (and more importantly) promote this book? What other books have you written? What are your credentials?

Competition: What other books on the subject exist and why is yours better than the rest?

Delivery information: anticipated word count (you should find out how many words they usually publish and go for that), anticipated time required to complete etc.

Your Platform: Do you already have a fan base? How many people are on your mailing list? How many visitors does your blog get? How many people make up your online social network? What other platforms, groups and clubs do you belong to or run?

Your Marketing Plan: How do you intend to reach your target audience? Are you planning to invest your own time and money into marketing your book? Will you be writing and giving away articles? Do you have a good media list? What specific marketing skills do you bring? Will you be doing public speaking? Are you planning to buy lots of books to sell direct? Are you prepared to take full responsibility for marketing? Do you have a large email list/twitter following/Facebook list (In case you haven't worked it out, the publisher would like your answer to be yes to most, if not all of these.)

Your synopsis should be riveting, exciting and interesting while making it clear where the market is.

A sample of your book

Publishers' requirements vary here: some will want to see a table of contents and a single chapter (to see how you write) while others request up to five chapters.

You will often have to format this differently for different publishers so follow their guidelines or ask for their guidelines if you can't find any.

Summary

You now have a clear idea of the routes you can choose to get your book published and the pros and cons of each: traditional publishing, self-publishing and hybrid publishing. You have been warned about scam 'self-publishing' companies, even those attached to big traditional publishing companies, and you should do due diligence on any publishers you are paying.

You can format your manuscript to meet the standards of the fussiest editors and are aware that you should follow to the letter the submission guidelines of each publisher.

Your covering letter, synopsis and sample of your manuscript will be full of the right information to sell your business or self-help book to the traditional or hybrid publishers you have selected to approach.

GET TO IT!

We wish you good luck with writing and publishing your business or self-help book and hope you now feel equipped to get through the whole process with the minimum of fuss. If you want to ask us for more advice, please get in touch. We promise you impartial advice – we won't try to sell to you.

Contact us through our website
http://www.rethinkpress.com

Our blog is full of extra information and you can download a free copy of our e-book *Publish Pathway* with even more information on the different routes to publication. We're also on social media and would love to be in contact with you on:

Facebook
http://www.facebook.com/RethinkPress

Twitter
http://www.twitter.com/RethinkPress

Or you can email us at

lucy@rethinkpress.com

And look out for our workshops, events and contributions to Key Person of Influence events and programmes
http://www.keypersonofinfluence.com

THE AUTHORS

Joe Gregory's background is in advertising as a graphic designer and copywriter. He started his first business in 1997 (aged 19) specialising in online marketing, branding and promotion. In 2003, Joe co-wrote *The Gorillas Want Bananas*, sharing his Lean Marketing approach. The success of this self-published book led to the creation of Bookshaker – an independent publishing business which has helped hundreds of coaches, consultants, trainers and expert business owners get their work published. Joe pioneered the current trend for entrepreneurs and small business owners to write and publish books that bring business in his second book, *The Wealthy Author*. He founded the hybrid publisher, Rethink Press, with Lucy in 2011 and is the Managing Publisher.

Lucy McCarraher started her first publishing company while she was at university. She is Managing Editor of Rethink Press and Bookshaker publishing, which have between them published over 350 niche business, self-development books and new fiction. Lucy is the Publish Mentor for Key Person of Influence UK and Singapore. She is the author of three novels and five self-help books, including *A Simpler Life*, *The Real Secret* and *How To Write Fiction Without The Fuss*. She is a highly experienced editor and writing coach, has worked with many writers in all genres to develop, polish and successfully publish their books. Lucy has a post-grad diploma in teaching Creative Writing and Literacy, and gives regular talks and workshops on writing and publishing.

49105696R00104

Made in the USA
Middletown, DE
05 October 2017